Melting Down

Writers of the Round Table Press
PO Box 511
Highland Park, IL 60035

Story Adaptation	NADJA BAER
Illustration	NATHAN LUETH
Publisher	COREY MICHAEL BLAKE
Executive Editor	KATIE GUTIERREZ
Creative Director	DAVID CHARLES COHEN
Post Production	DAVID CHARLES COHEN
Directoress of Happiness	ERIN COHEN
Director of Author Services	KRISTIN WESTBERG
Facts Keeper	MIKE WINICOUR
Front Cover Design	NATHAN LUETH, SUNNY DIMARTINO
Interior Design and Layout	SUNNY DIMARTINO
Proofreading	RITA HESS
Last Looks	JESS PLACE
Digital Book Conversion	SUNNY DIMARTINO
Digital Publishing	SUNNY DIMARTINO

Printed in the United States of America

First Edition: April 2013
10 9 8 7 6 5 4 3 2

Library of Congress Cataloging-in-Publication Data
Krukar, Jeff
Melting down: a comic for kids with asperger's disorder and
challenging behavior / Jeff Krukar and Katie Gutierrez
with James G. Balestrieri.—1st ed. p. cm.
Print ISBN: 978-1-939418-20-3   Digital ISBN: 978-1-939418-21-0
Library of Congress Control Number: 2013935902
Number 2 in the series: The ORP Library
The ORP Library: Melting Down

Melting Down

A COMIC FOR KIDS WITH ASPERGER'S DISORDER AND CHALLENGING BEHAVIOR

THE ORP LIBRARY

WRITTEN BY **JEFF KRUKAR, PH.D.**
KATIE GUTIERREZ

WITH **JAMES G. BALESTRIERI**

ADAPTED BY **NADJA BAER**

ILLUSTRATED BY **NATHAN LUETH**

Introduction

I have led Oconomowoc Residential Programs (ORP) for almost thirty years. We're a family of companies offering specialized services and care for children, adolescents, and adults with disabilities. Too often, when parents of children with disabilities try to find funding for programs like ours, they are bombarded by red tape, conflicting information, or no information at all, so they struggle blindly for years to secure an appropriate education. Meanwhile, home life, and the child's wellbeing, suffers. In cases when parents and caretakers have exhausted their options—and their hope—ORP is here to help. We felt it was time to offer parents a new, unexpected tool to fight back: stories that educate, empower, and inspire.

The original idea was to create a library of comic books that could empower families with information to reclaim their rights. We wanted to give parents and caretakers the information they need to advocate for themselves, as well as provide educators and therapists with a therapeutic tool. And, of course, we wanted to reach the children—to offer them a visual representation of their journey that would show that they aren't alone, nor are they wrong or "bad" for their differences.

What we found in the process of writing original stories for the comics is that these journeys are too long, too complex, to be contained within a standard comic. So what we are now creating is an ORP library of disabilities books—traditional books geared toward parents, caretakers, educators, and therapists, *and* comic books like this one that portray the world through the eyes of children with disabilities. Both styles of books share what we have learned while advocating for families over the years while also honestly highlighting their emotional journeys.

In an ideal situation, this companion children's book will be used therapeutically, to communicate directly with these amazing children, and to help support the work ORP and companies like ours are doing. These books are the best I have to offer and if they even help a handful of people the effort will have been worth it.

Sincerely,

Jim Balestrieri
CEO, Oconomowoc Residential Programs

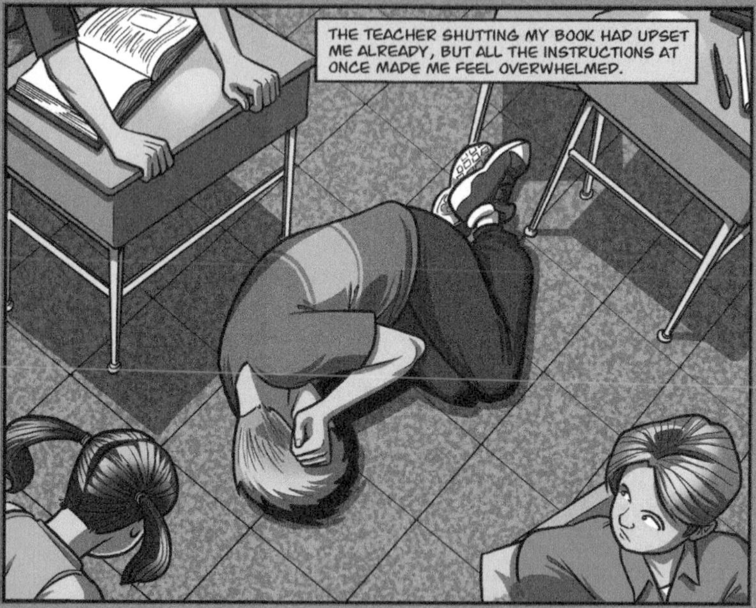
THE TEACHER SHUTTING MY BOOK HAD UPSET ME ALREADY, BUT ALL THE INSTRUCTIONS AT ONCE MADE ME FEEL OVERWHELMED.

A Note About This Book

Asperger's disorder is a complex syndrome that affects children in different ways. The child with Asperger's disorder depicted in the following story struggles with significant emotional and behavioral difficulties that require a therapeutic environment. The great majority of children with Asperger's disorder do not resemble the child shown in this story. But those who do resemble him face challenges that have made it difficult to benefit from education in the public school system. At Genesee Lake School, we strive to build relationships with the children in our care so that they learn new skills that will lead to a successful return to their home, school, and community. It is our hope that the following story will add to your own understanding of the often lonely journey experienced by families with children with these unique challenges and gifts.

I'M NOT SURE WHEN I FIRST REALIZED THAT I WAS A LITTLE DIFFERENT, BUT EVERYONE ELSE ALWAYS SEEMED TO KNOW. I DO REMEMBER THAT DETAILS WERE VERY IMPORTANT TO ME, AND THAT WHENEVER SOMEONE CHANGED THINGS ON ME, I GOT VERY UPSET.

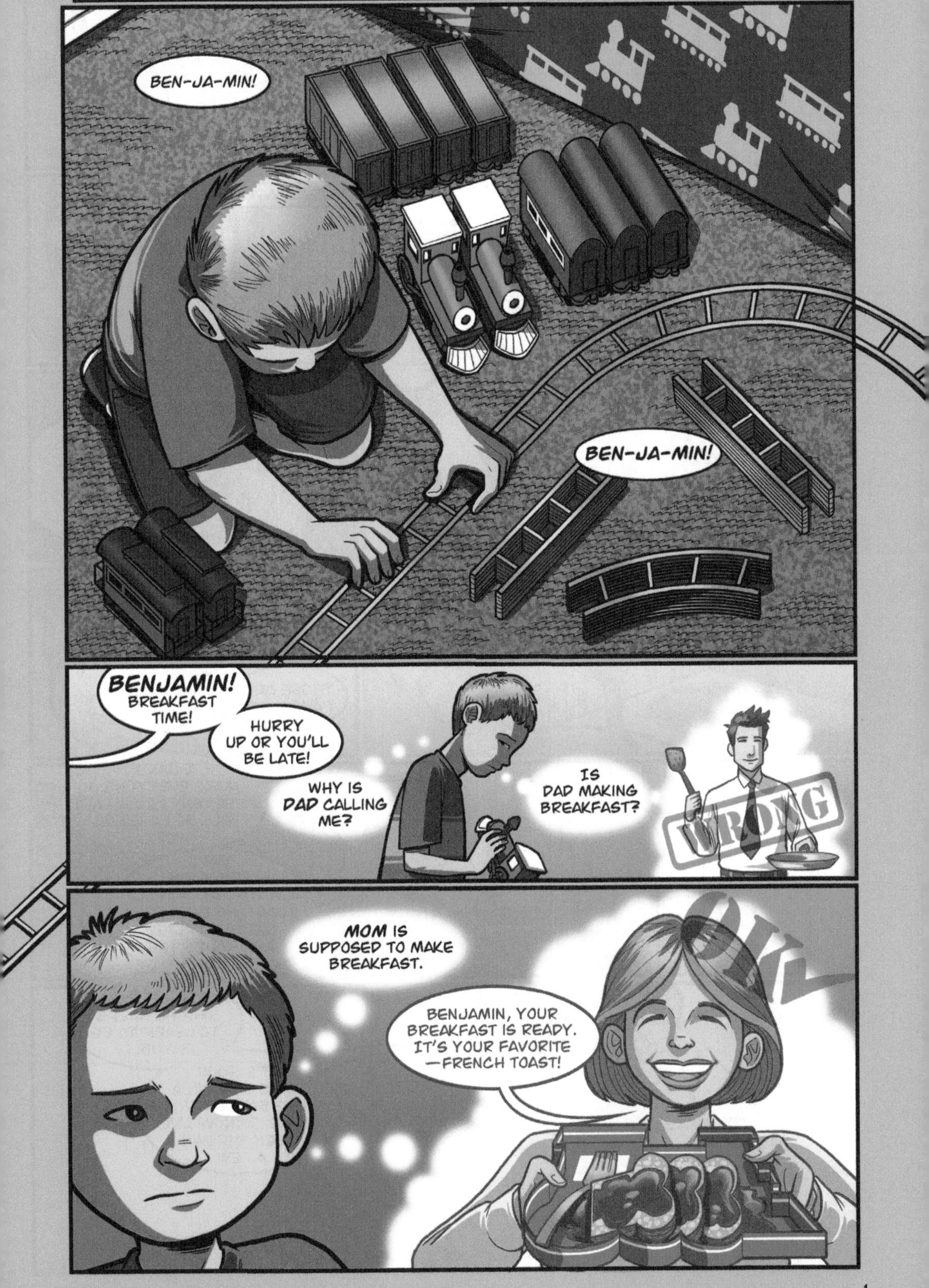
BEN-JA-MIN!
BEN-JA-MIN!
BENJAMIN! BREAKFAST TIME!
HURRY UP OR YOU'LL BE LATE!
WHY IS DAD CALLING ME?
IS DAD MAKING BREAKFAST?
WRONG
MOM IS SUPPOSED TO MAKE BREAKFAST.
BENJAMIN, YOUR BREAKFAST IS READY. IT'S YOUR FAVORITE —FRENCH TOAST!

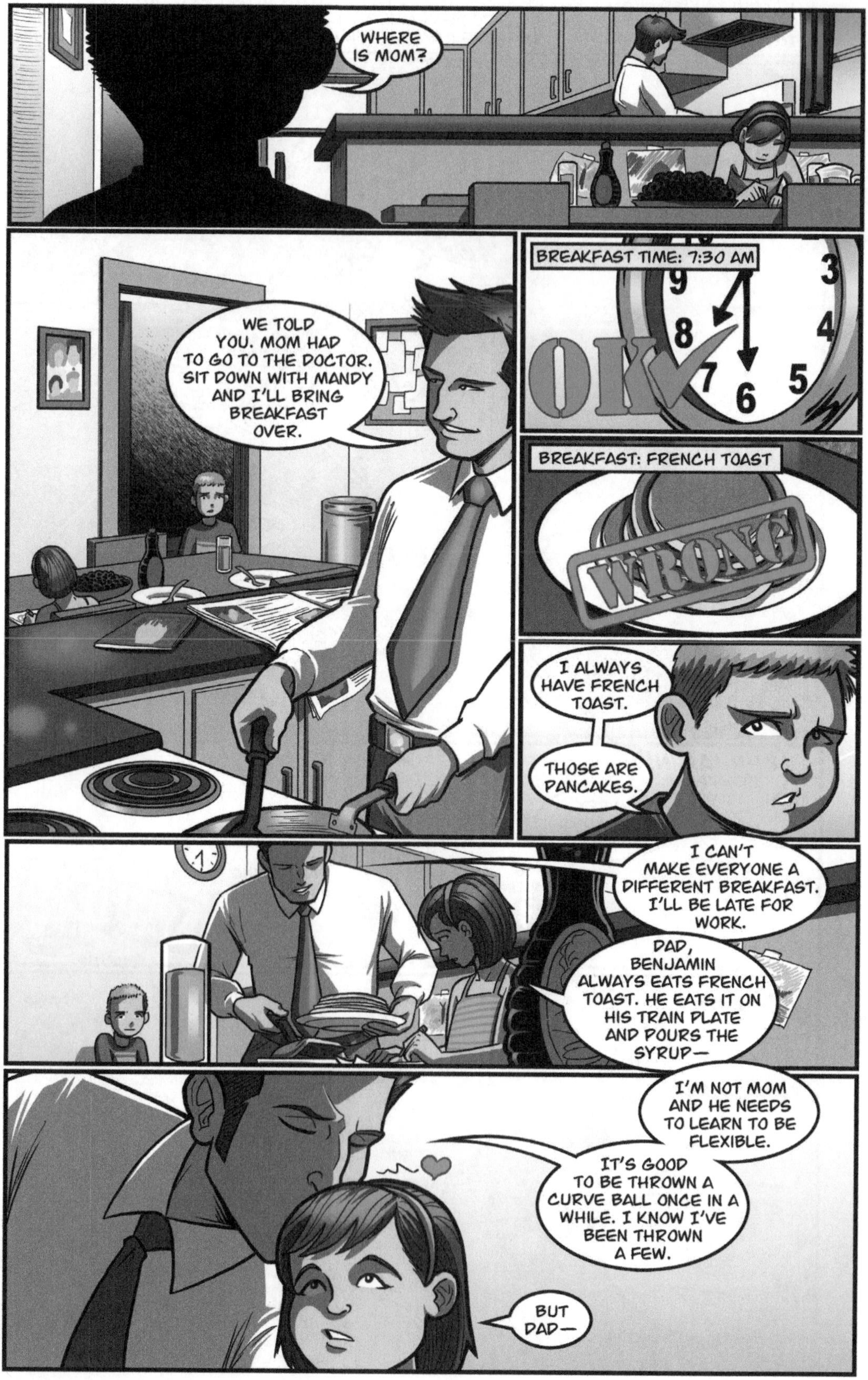
WHERE IS MOM?
WE TOLD YOU. MOM HAD TO GO TO THE DOCTOR. SIT DOWN WITH MANDY AND I'LL BRING BREAKFAST OVER.
BREAKFAST TIME: 7:30 AM
OK
BREAKFAST: FRENCH TOAST
WRONG
I ALWAYS HAVE FRENCH TOAST.
THOSE ARE PANCAKES.
I CAN'T MAKE EVERYONE A DIFFERENT BREAKFAST. I'LL BE LATE FOR WORK.
DAD, BENJAMIN ALWAYS EATS FRENCH TOAST. HE EATS IT ON HIS TRAIN PLATE AND POURS THE SYRUP—
I'M NOT MOM AND HE NEEDS TO LEARN TO BE FLEXIBLE.
IT'S GOOD TO BE THROWN A CURVE BALL ONCE IN A WHILE. I KNOW I'VE BEEN THROWN A FEW.
BUT DAD—

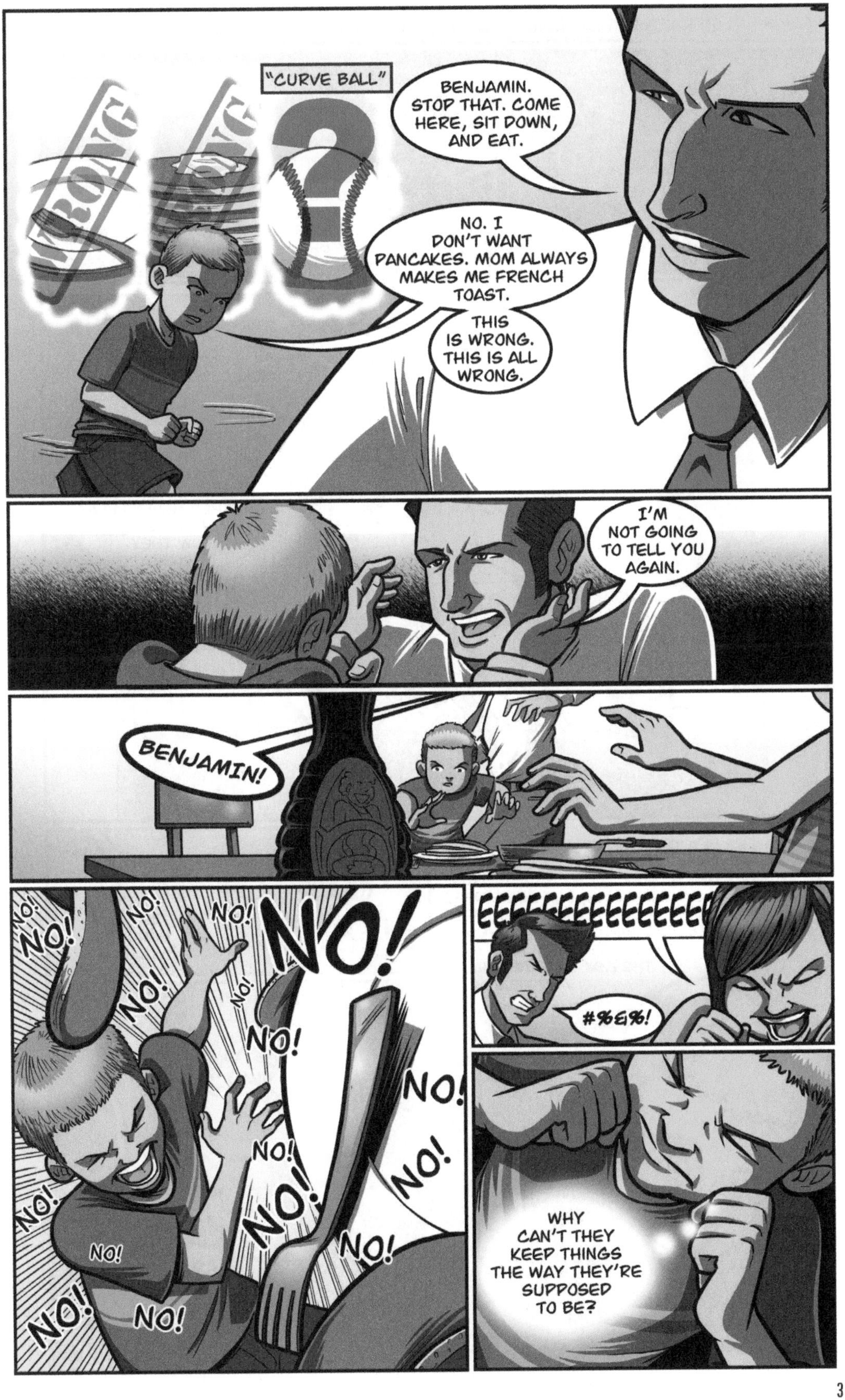
"CURVE BALL"
WRONG
WRONG
BENJAMIN. STOP THAT. COME HERE, SIT DOWN, AND EAT.
NO. I DON'T WANT PANCAKES. MOM ALWAYS MAKES ME FRENCH TOAST.
THIS IS WRONG. THIS IS ALL WRONG.
I'M NOT GOING TO TELL YOU AGAIN.
BENJAMIN!
NO! NO! NO! NO! NO!
NO!
NO! NO! NO! NO! NO! NO! NO! NO! NO! NO! NO! NO!
EEEEEEEEEEEEEEEE
#%&%!
WHY CAN'T THEY KEEP THINGS THE WAY THEY'RE SUPPOSED TO BE?

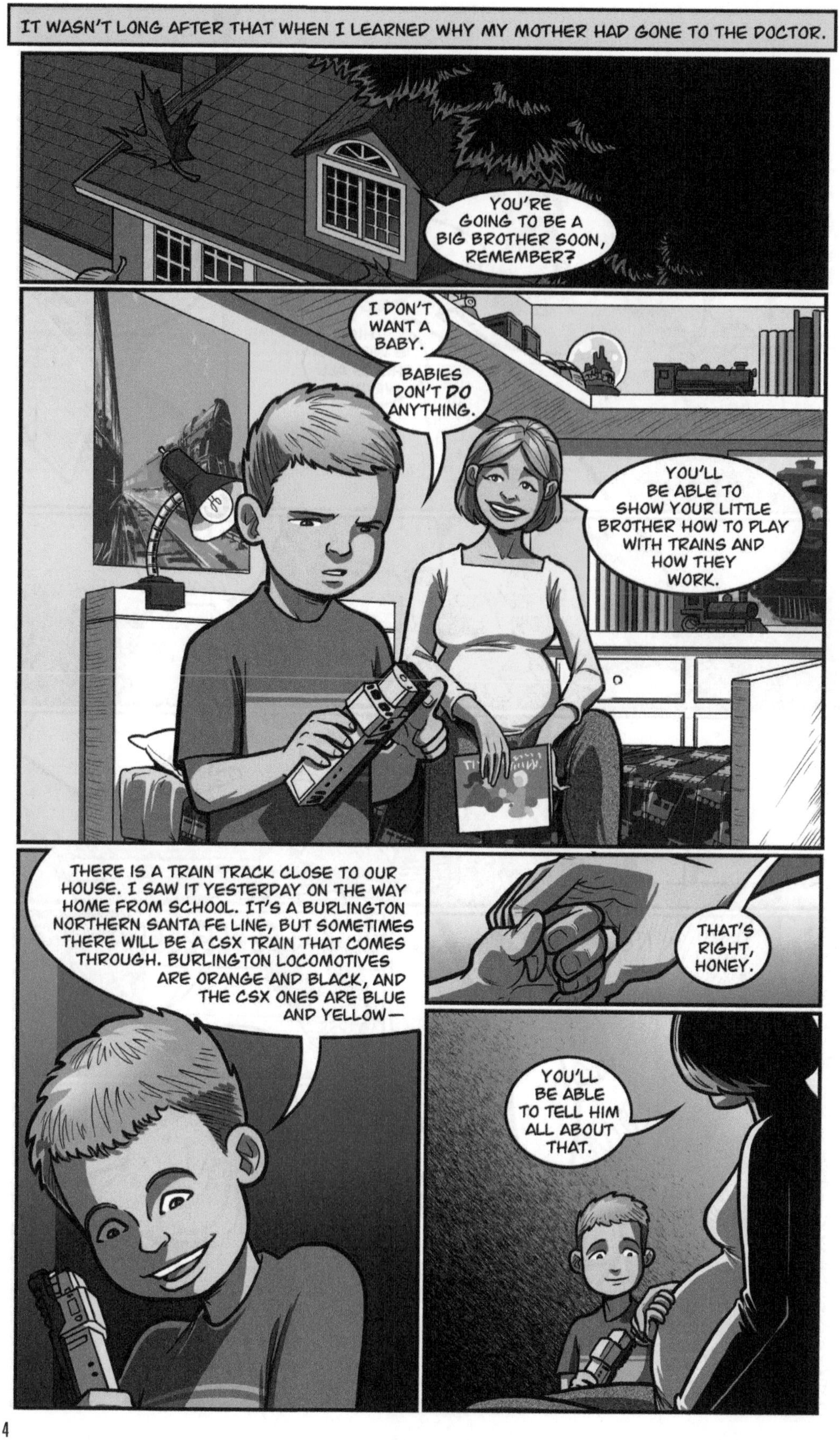
IT WASN'T LONG AFTER THAT WHEN I LEARNED WHY MY MOTHER HAD GONE TO THE DOCTOR.
YOU'RE GOING TO BE A BIG BROTHER SOON, REMEMBER?
I DON'T WANT A BABY.
BABIES DON'T *DO* ANYTHING.
YOU'LL BE ABLE TO SHOW YOUR LITTLE BROTHER HOW TO PLAY WITH TRAINS AND HOW THEY WORK.
THERE IS A TRAIN TRACK CLOSE TO OUR HOUSE. I SAW IT YESTERDAY ON THE WAY HOME FROM SCHOOL. IT'S A BURLINGTON NORTHERN SANTA FE LINE, BUT SOMETIMES THERE WILL BE A CSX TRAIN THAT COMES THROUGH. BURLINGTON LOCOMOTIVES ARE ORANGE AND BLACK, AND THE CSX ONES ARE BLUE AND YELLOW—
THAT'S RIGHT, HONEY.
YOU'LL BE ABLE TO TELL HIM ALL ABOUT THAT.

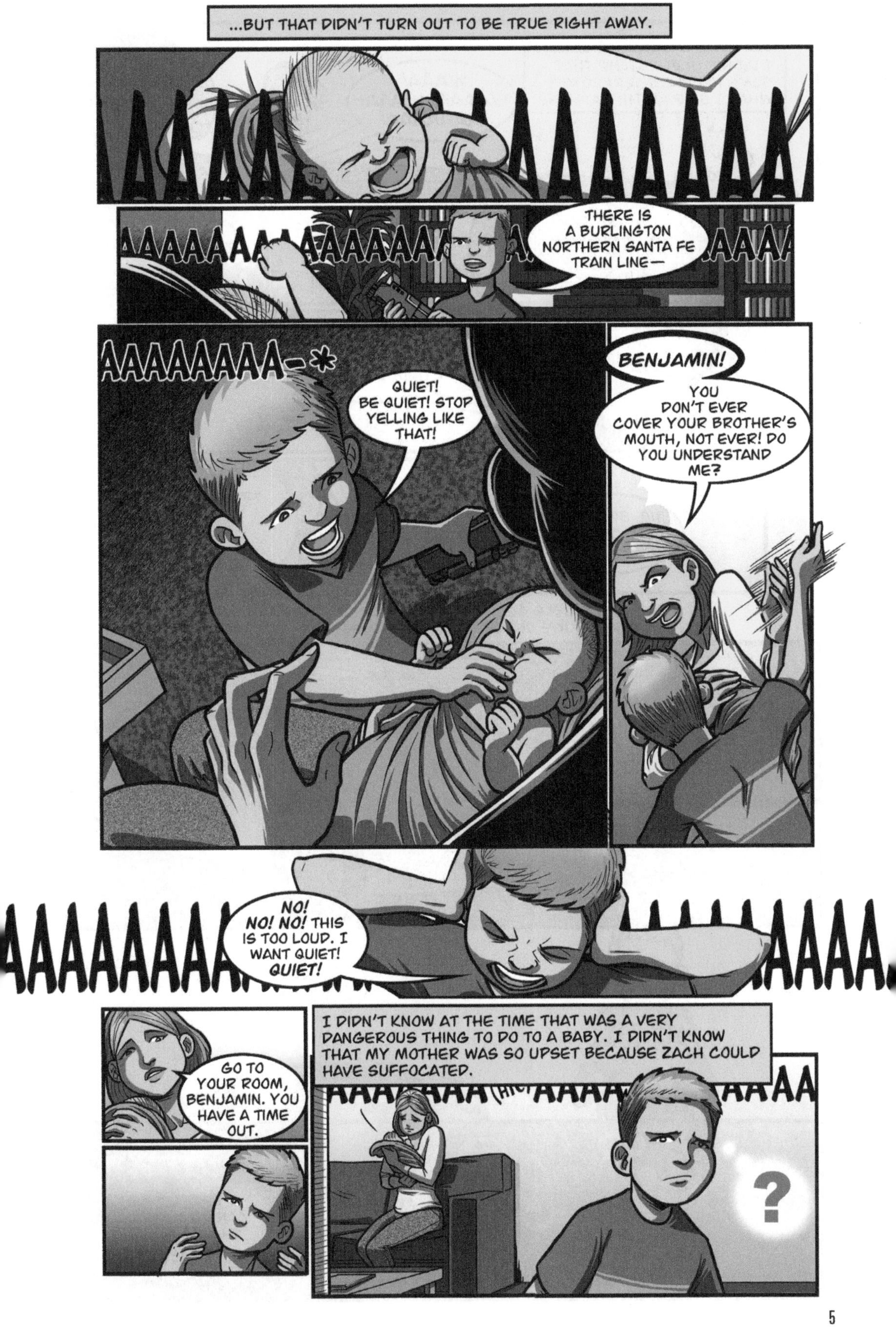

...BUT THAT DIDN'T TURN OUT TO BE TRUE RIGHT AWAY.
AAAAAAAAAAAAAAAA
THERE IS A BURLINGTON NORTHERN SANTA FE TRAIN LINE—
AAAAAAAAAAAAAAAAAAAAAA
AAAAAAAAA-*
QUIET! BE QUIET! STOP YELLING LIKE THAT!
BENJAMIN!
YOU DON'T EVER COVER YOUR BROTHER'S MOUTH, NOT EVER! DO YOU UNDERSTAND ME?
NO! NO! NO! THIS IS TOO LOUD. I WANT QUIET! QUIET!
GO TO YOUR ROOM, BENJAMIN. YOU HAVE A TIME OUT.
I DIDN'T KNOW AT THE TIME THAT WAS A VERY DANGEROUS THING TO DO TO A BABY. I DIDN'T KNOW THAT MY MOTHER WAS SO UPSET BECAUSE ZACH COULD HAVE SUFFOCATED.
?

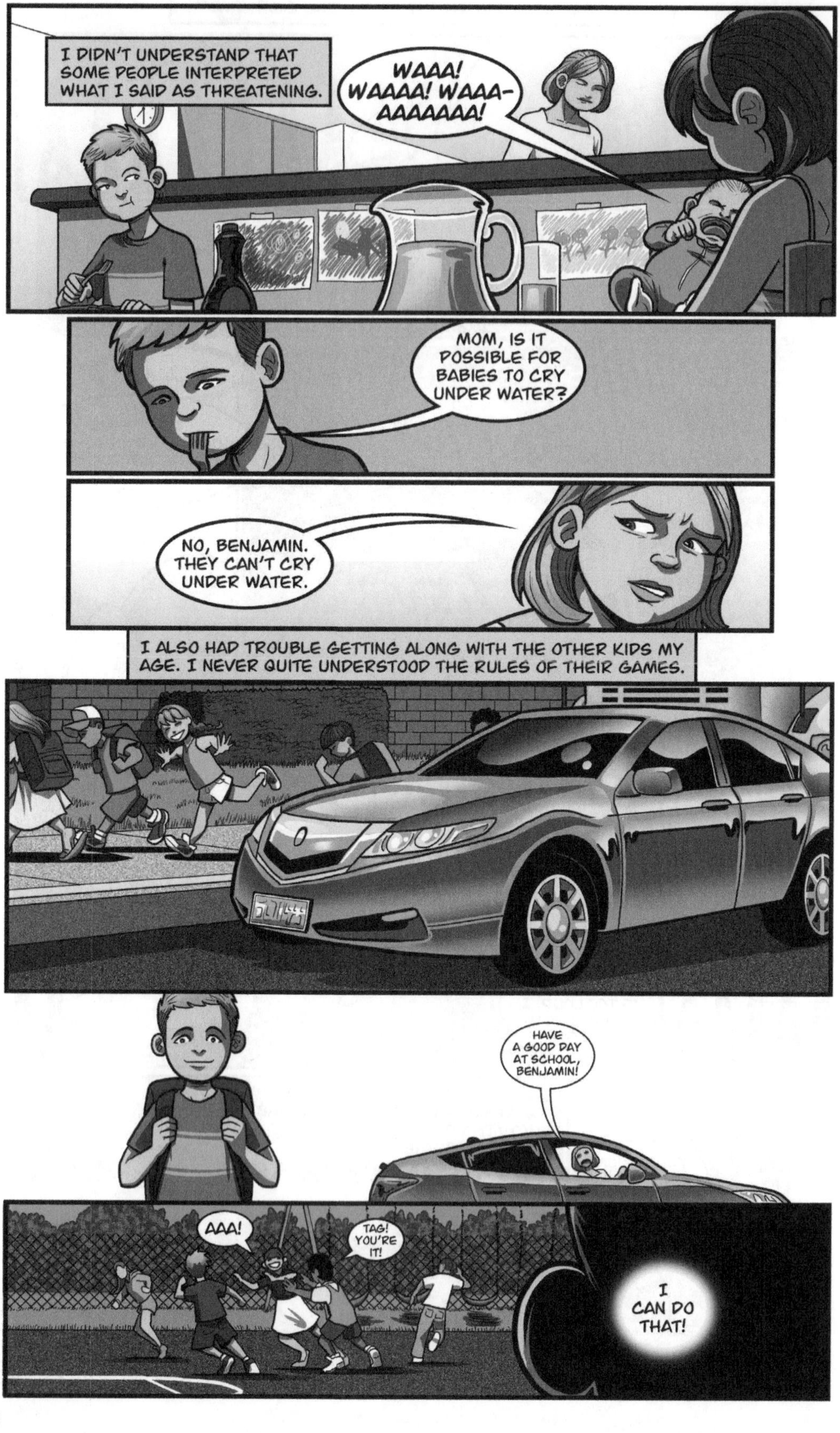

I DIDN'T UNDERSTAND THAT SOME PEOPLE INTERPRETED WHAT I SAID AS THREATENING.
WAAA! WAAAA! WAAA-AAAAAAA!
MOM, IS IT POSSIBLE FOR BABIES TO CRY UNDER WATER?
NO, BENJAMIN. THEY CAN'T CRY UNDER WATER.
I ALSO HAD TROUBLE GETTING ALONG WITH THE OTHER KIDS MY AGE. I NEVER QUITE UNDERSTOOD THE RULES OF THEIR GAMES.
HAVE A GOOD DAY AT SCHOOL, BENJAMIN!
AAA!
TAG! YOU'RE IT!
I CAN DO THAT!

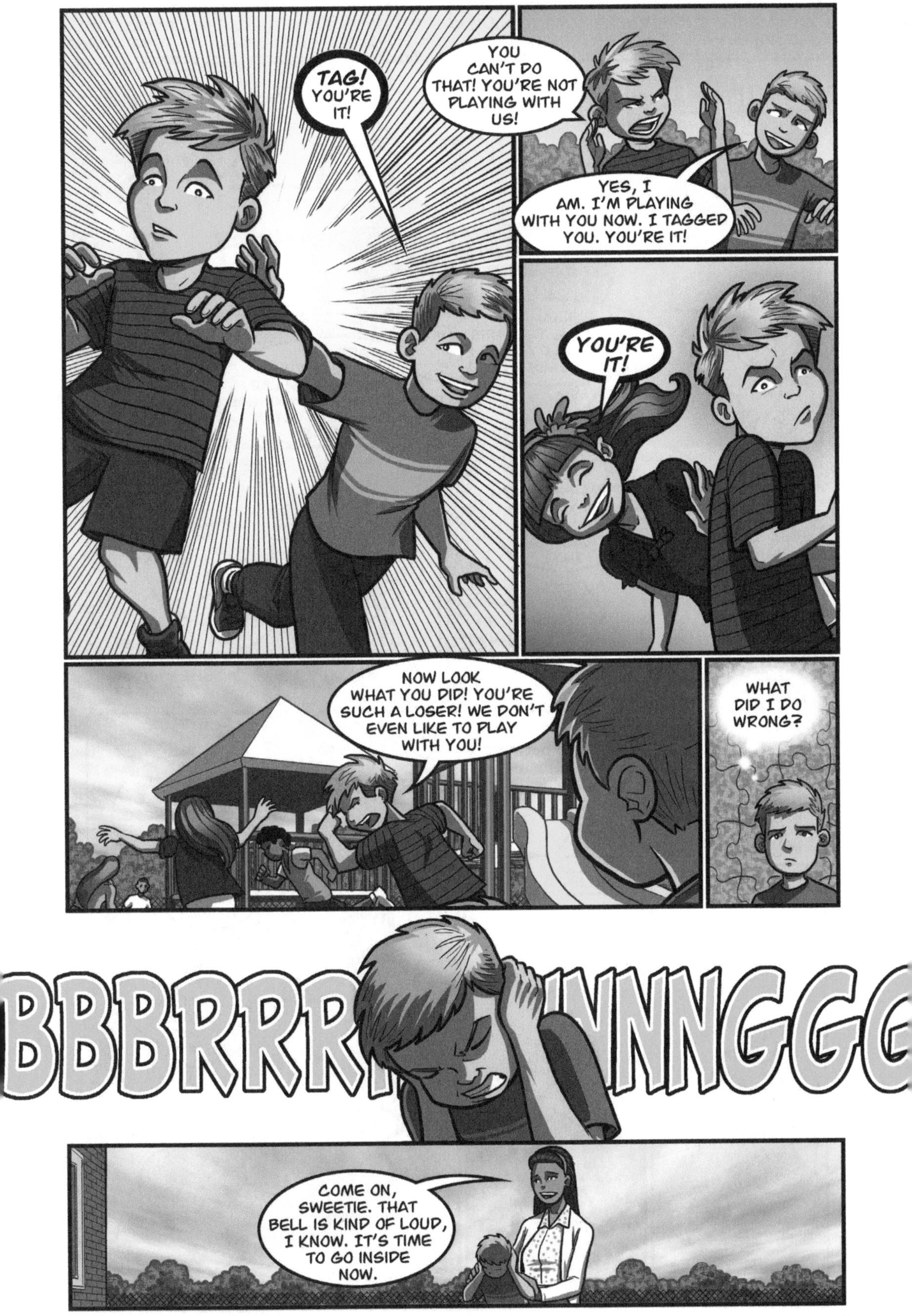
TAG! YOU'RE IT!
YOU CAN'T DO THAT! YOU'RE NOT PLAYING WITH US!
YES, I AM. I'M PLAYING WITH YOU NOW. I TAGGED YOU. YOU'RE IT!
YOU'RE IT!
NOW LOOK WHAT YOU DID! YOU'RE SUCH A LOSER! WE DON'T EVEN LIKE TO PLAY WITH YOU!
WHAT DID I DO WRONG?
COME ON, SWEETIE. THAT BELL IS KIND OF LOUD, I KNOW. IT'S TIME TO GO INSIDE NOW.

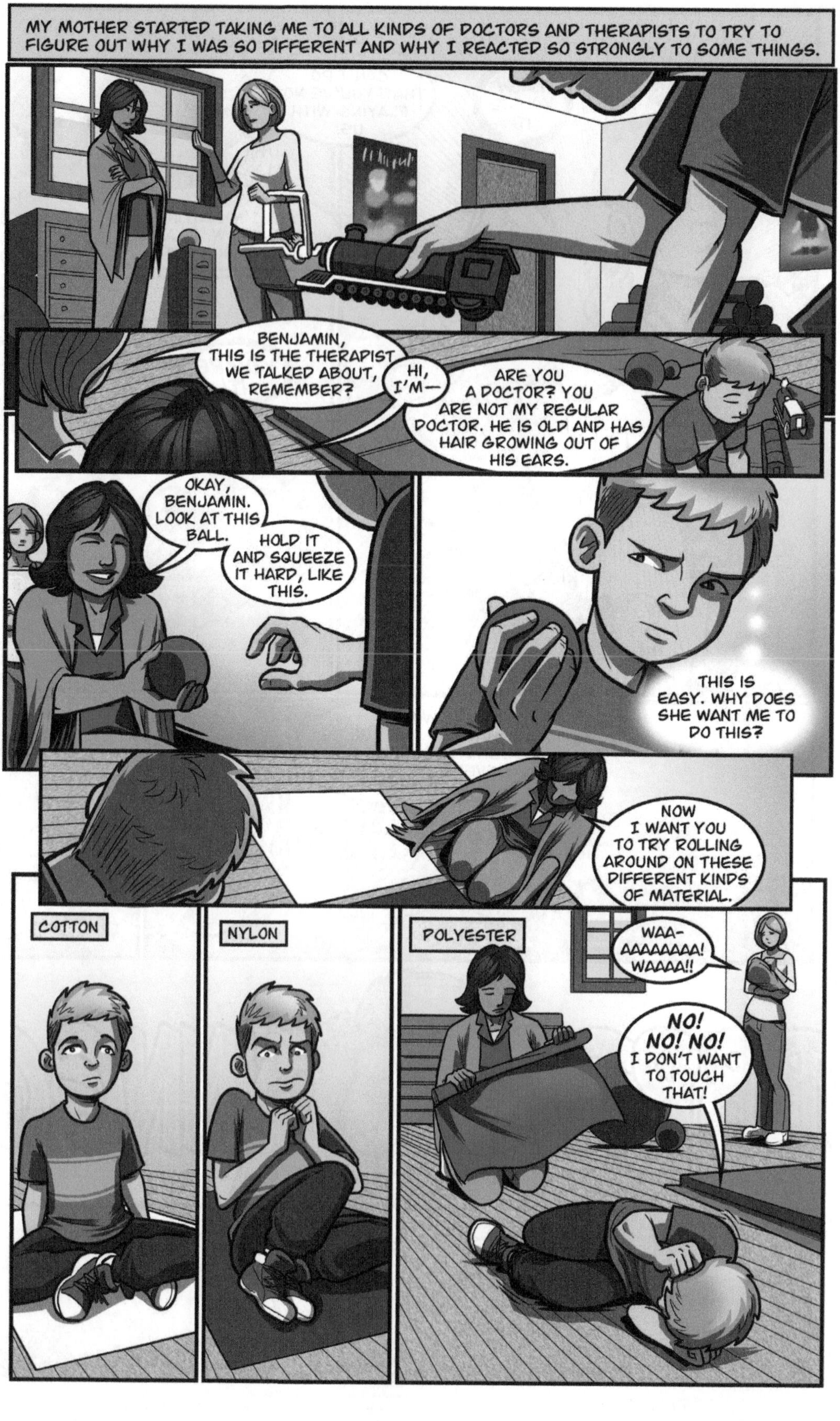
MY MOTHER STARTED TAKING ME TO ALL KINDS OF DOCTORS AND THERAPISTS TO TRY TO FIGURE OUT WHY I WAS SO DIFFERENT AND WHY I REACTED SO STRONGLY TO SOME THINGS.
BENJAMIN, THIS IS THE THERAPIST WE TALKED ABOUT, REMEMBER?
HI, I'M—
ARE YOU A DOCTOR? YOU ARE NOT MY REGULAR DOCTOR. HE IS OLD AND HAS HAIR GROWING OUT OF HIS EARS.
OKAY, BENJAMIN. LOOK AT THIS BALL.
HOLD IT AND SQUEEZE IT HARD, LIKE THIS.
THIS IS EASY. WHY DOES SHE WANT ME TO DO THIS?
NOW I WANT YOU TO TRY ROLLING AROUND ON THESE DIFFERENT KINDS OF MATERIAL.
COTTON
NYLON
POLYESTER
WAA-AAAAAAAA! WAAAA!!
NO! NO! NO! I DON'T WANT TO TOUCH THAT!

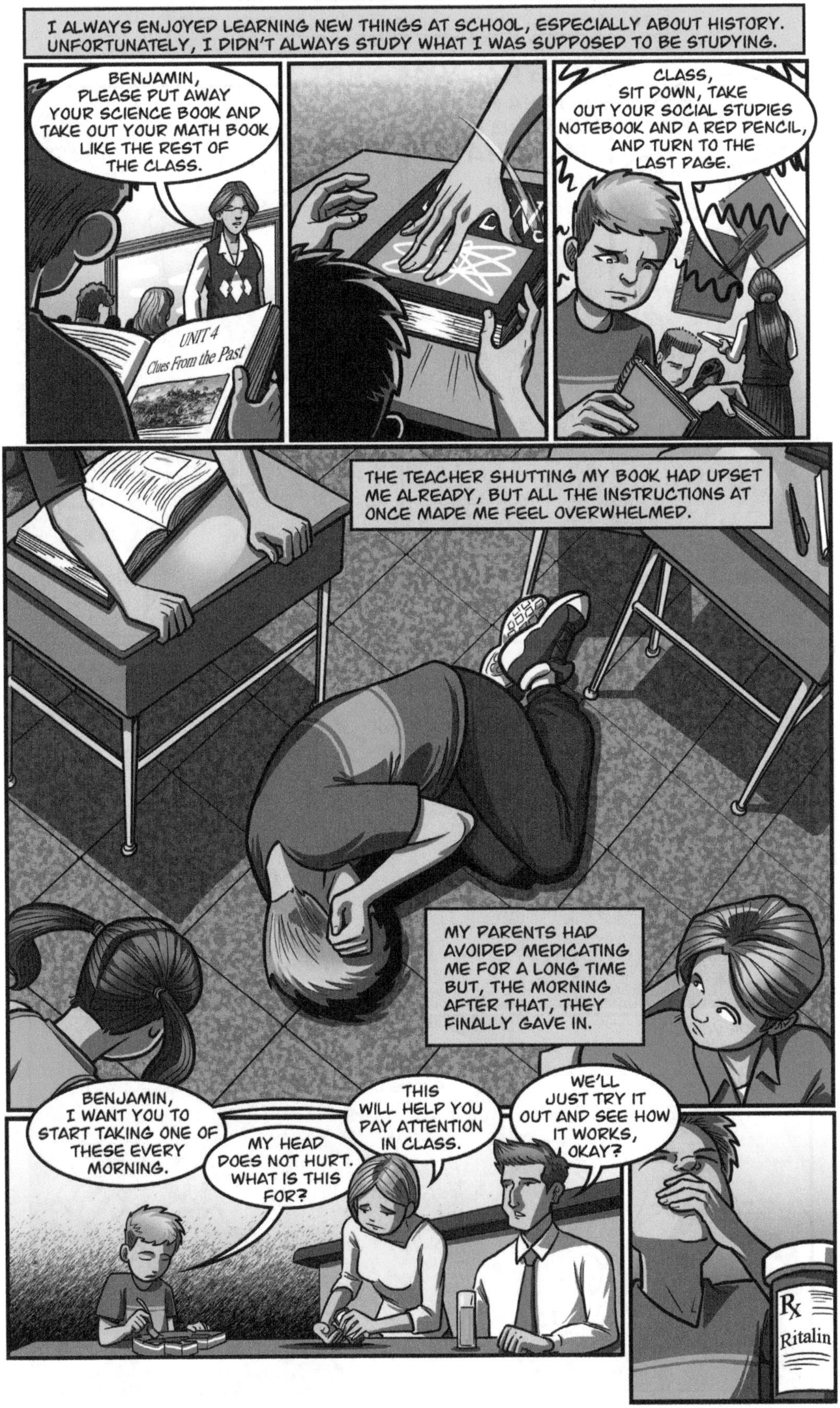
I ALWAYS ENJOYED LEARNING NEW THINGS AT SCHOOL, ESPECIALLY ABOUT HISTORY. UNFORTUNATELY, I DIDN'T ALWAYS STUDY WHAT I WAS SUPPOSED TO BE STUDYING.
BENJAMIN, PLEASE PUT AWAY YOUR SCIENCE BOOK AND TAKE OUT YOUR MATH BOOK LIKE THE REST OF THE CLASS.
UNIT 4
Clues From the Past
CLASS, SIT DOWN, TAKE OUT YOUR SOCIAL STUDIES NOTEBOOK AND A RED PENCIL, AND TURN TO THE LAST PAGE.
THE TEACHER SHUTTING MY BOOK HAD UPSET ME ALREADY, BUT ALL THE INSTRUCTIONS AT ONCE MADE ME FEEL OVERWHELMED.
MY PARENTS HAD AVOIDED MEDICATING ME FOR A LONG TIME BUT, THE MORNING AFTER THAT, THEY FINALLY GAVE IN.
BENJAMIN, I WANT YOU TO START TAKING ONE OF THESE EVERY MORNING.
MY HEAD DOES NOT HURT. WHAT IS THIS FOR?
THIS WILL HELP YOU PAY ATTENTION IN CLASS.
WE'LL JUST TRY IT OUT AND SEE HOW IT WORKS, OKAY?
Rx
Ritalin

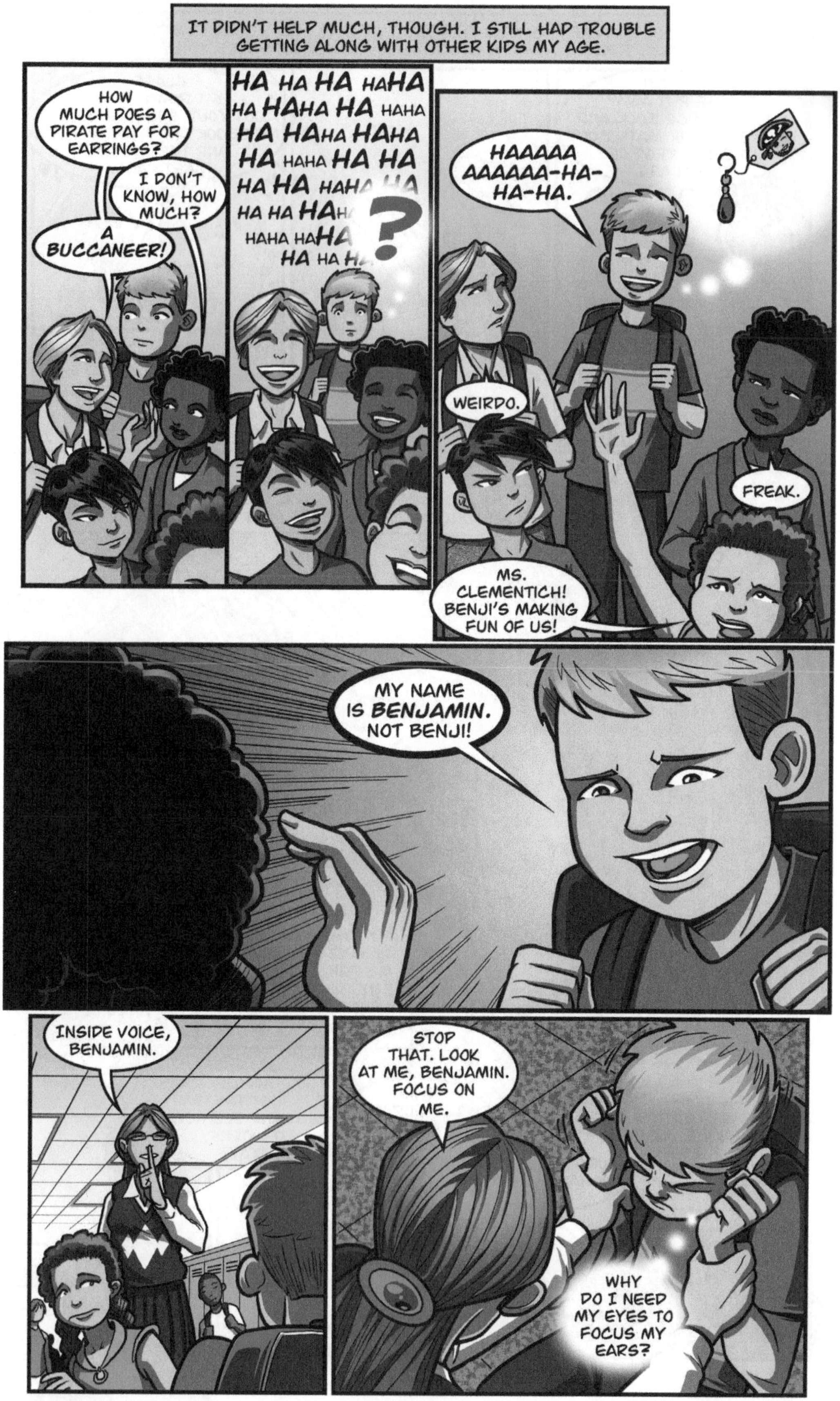
IT DIDN'T HELP MUCH, THOUGH. I STILL HAD TROUBLE GETTING ALONG WITH OTHER KIDS MY AGE.
HOW MUCH DOES A PIRATE PAY FOR EARRINGS?
I DON'T KNOW, HOW MUCH?
A BUCCANEER!
HA ha HA haHA
ha HAha HA haha
HA HAha HAha
HA haha HA HA
ha HA
ha ha HA
haha haHA
HA ha
?
HAAAAA AAAAAA-HA-HA-HA.
WEIRDO.
FREAK.
MS. CLEMENTICH! BENJI'S MAKING FUN OF US!
MY NAME IS BENJAMIN. NOT BENJI!
INSIDE VOICE, BENJAMIN.
STOP THAT. LOOK AT ME, BENJAMIN. FOCUS ON ME.
WHY DO I NEED MY EYES TO FOCUS MY EARS?

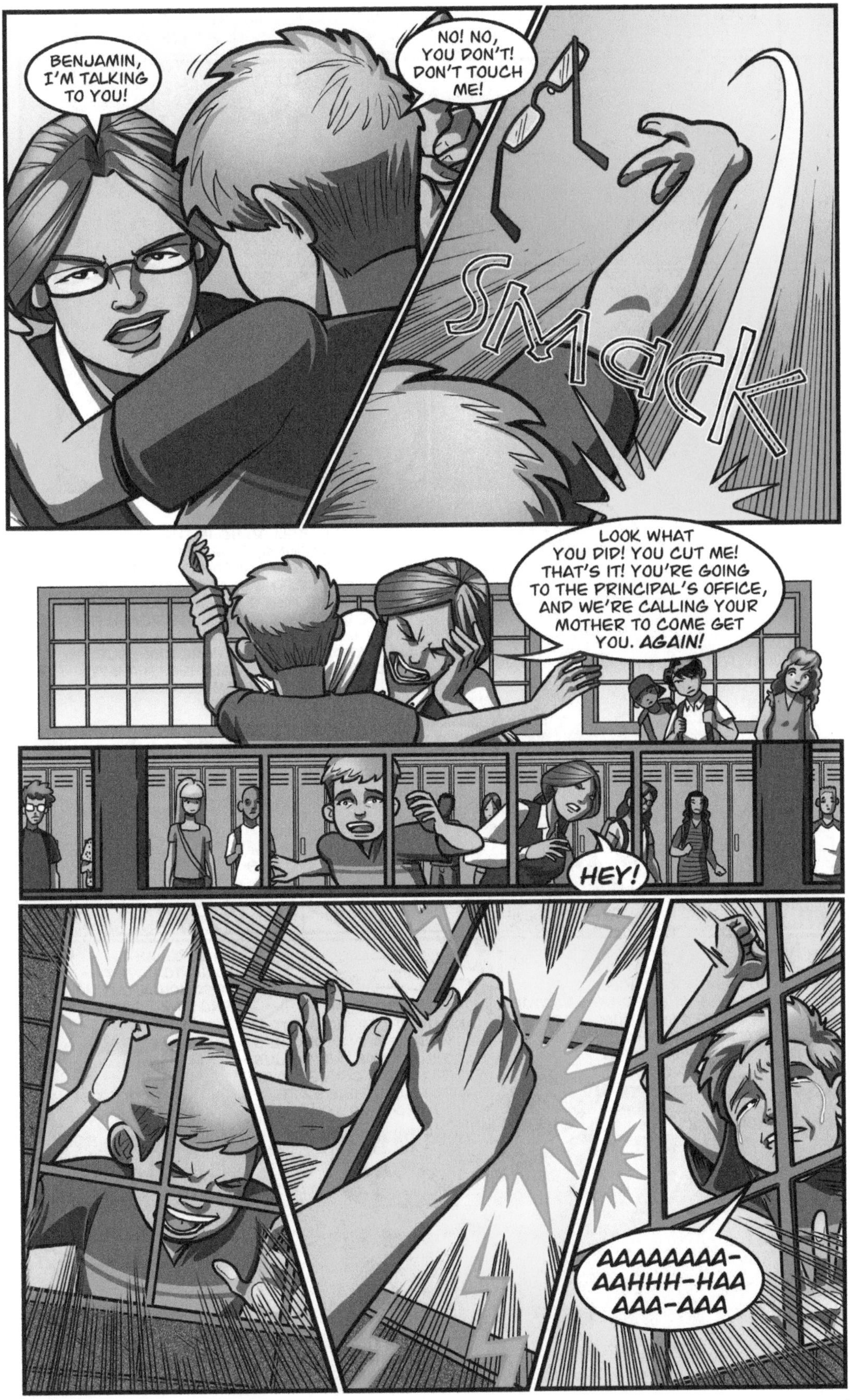
BENJAMIN, I'M TALKING TO YOU!
NO! NO, YOU DON'T! DON'T TOUCH ME!
SMACK
LOOK WHAT YOU DID! YOU CUT ME! THAT'S IT! YOU'RE GOING TO THE PRINCIPAL'S OFFICE, AND WE'RE CALLING YOUR MOTHER TO COME GET YOU. AGAIN!
HEY!
AAAAAAAA-AAHHH-HAA AAA-AAA

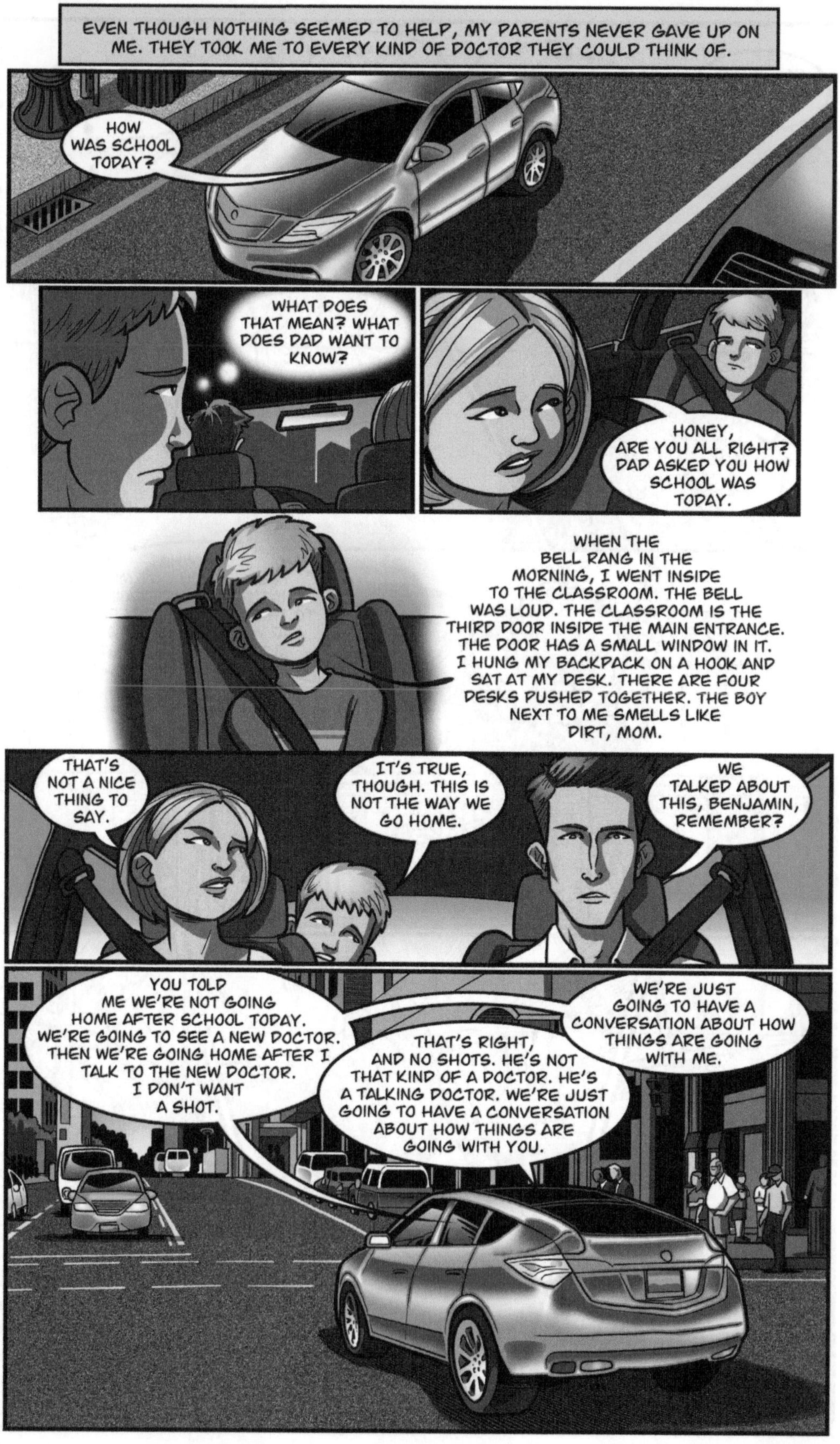
EVEN THOUGH NOTHING SEEMED TO HELP, MY PARENTS NEVER GAVE UP ON ME. THEY TOOK ME TO EVERY KIND OF DOCTOR THEY COULD THINK OF.
HOW WAS SCHOOL TODAY?
WHAT DOES THAT MEAN? WHAT DOES DAD WANT TO KNOW?
HONEY, ARE YOU ALL RIGHT? DAD ASKED YOU HOW SCHOOL WAS TODAY.
WHEN THE BELL RANG IN THE MORNING, I WENT INSIDE TO THE CLASSROOM. THE BELL WAS LOUD. THE CLASSROOM IS THE THIRD DOOR INSIDE THE MAIN ENTRANCE. THE DOOR HAS A SMALL WINDOW IN IT. I HUNG MY BACKPACK ON A HOOK AND SAT AT MY DESK. THERE ARE FOUR DESKS PUSHED TOGETHER. THE BOY NEXT TO ME SMELLS LIKE DIRT, MOM.
THAT'S NOT A NICE THING TO SAY.
IT'S TRUE, THOUGH. THIS IS NOT THE WAY WE GO HOME.
WE TALKED ABOUT THIS, BENJAMIN, REMEMBER?
YOU TOLD ME WE'RE NOT GOING HOME AFTER SCHOOL TODAY. WE'RE GOING TO SEE A NEW DOCTOR. THEN WE'RE GOING HOME AFTER I TALK TO THE NEW DOCTOR. I DON'T WANT A SHOT.
THAT'S RIGHT, AND NO SHOTS. HE'S NOT THAT KIND OF A DOCTOR. HE'S A TALKING DOCTOR. WE'RE JUST GOING TO HAVE A CONVERSATION ABOUT HOW THINGS ARE GOING WITH YOU.
WE'RE JUST GOING TO HAVE A CONVERSATION ABOUT HOW THINGS ARE GOING WITH ME.

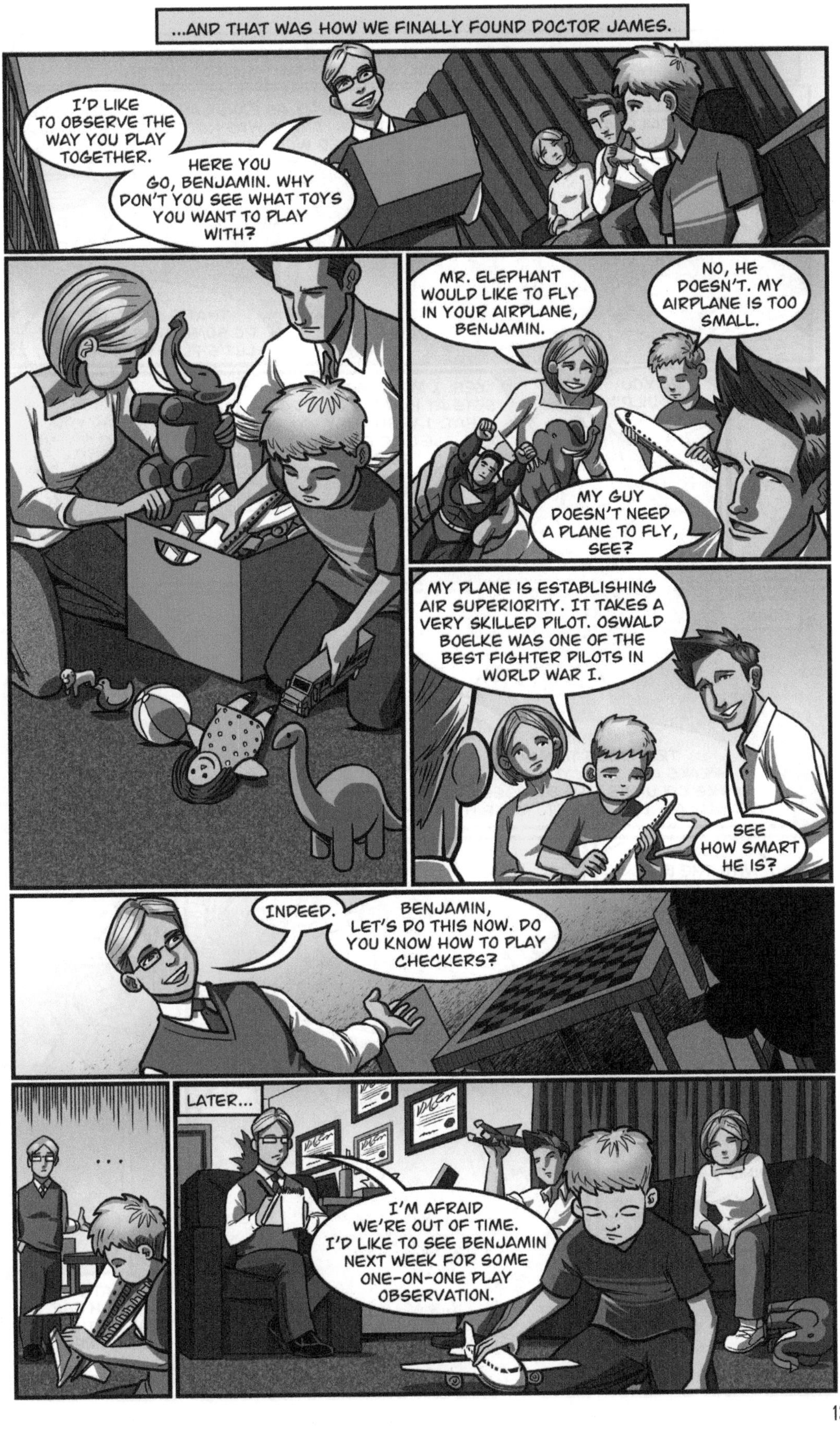
...AND THAT WAS HOW WE FINALLY FOUND DOCTOR JAMES.
I'D LIKE TO OBSERVE THE WAY YOU PLAY TOGETHER.
HERE YOU GO, BENJAMIN. WHY DON'T YOU SEE WHAT TOYS YOU WANT TO PLAY WITH?
MR. ELEPHANT WOULD LIKE TO FLY IN YOUR AIRPLANE, BENJAMIN.
NO, HE DOESN'T. MY AIRPLANE IS TOO SMALL.
MY GUY DOESN'T NEED A PLANE TO FLY, SEE?
MY PLANE IS ESTABLISHING AIR SUPERIORITY. IT TAKES A VERY SKILLED PILOT. OSWALD BOELKE WAS ONE OF THE BEST FIGHTER PILOTS IN WORLD WAR I.
SEE HOW SMART HE IS?
INDEED.
BENJAMIN, LET'S DO THIS NOW. DO YOU KNOW HOW TO PLAY CHECKERS?
...
LATER...
I'M AFRAID WE'RE OUT OF TIME. I'D LIKE TO SEE BENJAMIN NEXT WEEK FOR SOME ONE-ON-ONE PLAY OBSERVATION.

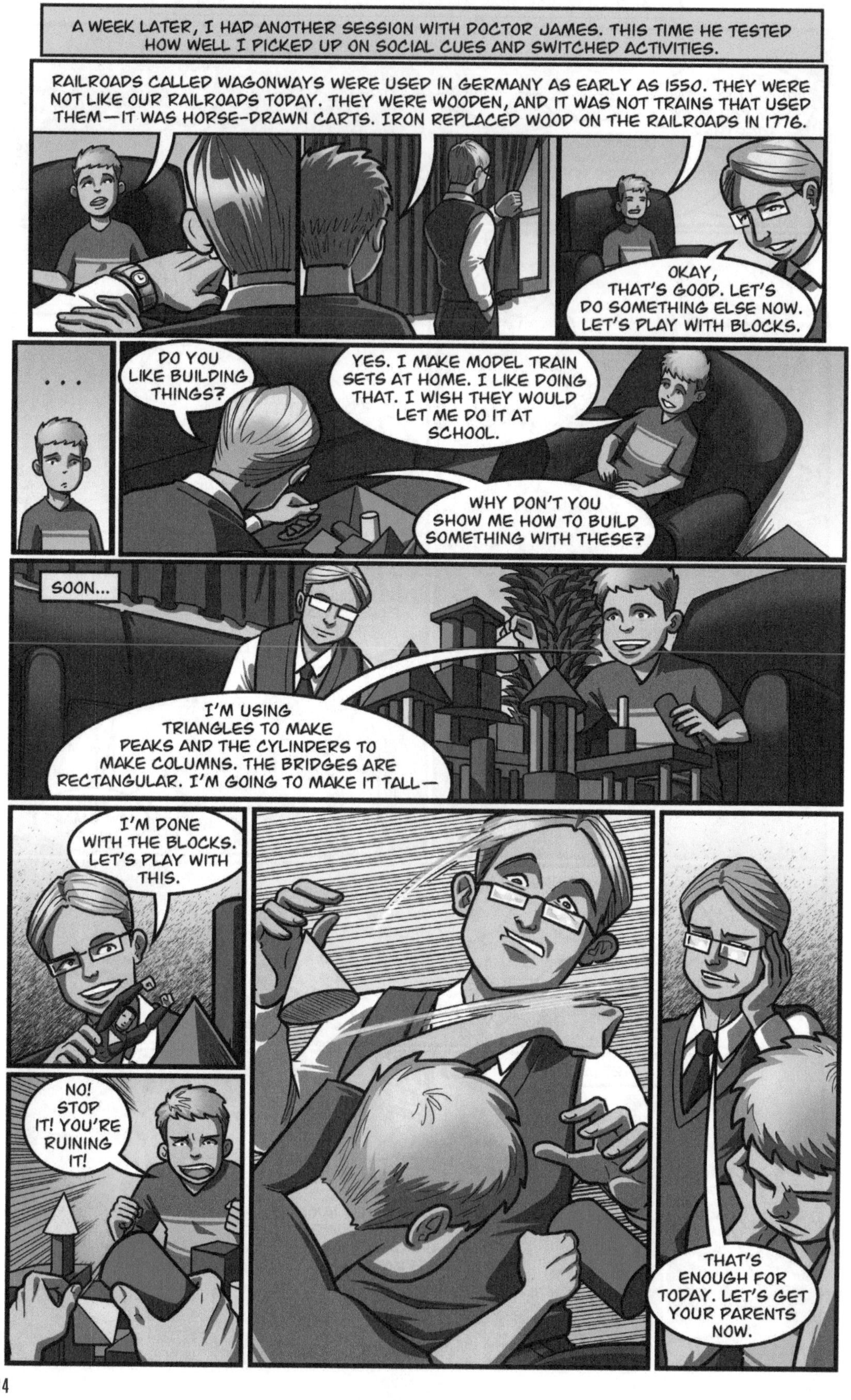
A WEEK LATER, I HAD ANOTHER SESSION WITH DOCTOR JAMES. THIS TIME HE TESTED HOW WELL I PICKED UP ON SOCIAL CUES AND SWITCHED ACTIVITIES.
RAILROADS CALLED WAGONWAYS WERE USED IN GERMANY AS EARLY AS 1550. THEY WERE NOT LIKE OUR RAILROADS TODAY. THEY WERE WOODEN, AND IT WAS NOT TRAINS THAT USED THEM—IT WAS HORSE-DRAWN CARTS. IRON REPLACED WOOD ON THE RAILROADS IN 1776.
OKAY, THAT'S GOOD. LET'S DO SOMETHING ELSE NOW. LET'S PLAY WITH BLOCKS.
. . .
DO YOU LIKE BUILDING THINGS?
YES. I MAKE MODEL TRAIN SETS AT HOME. I LIKE DOING THAT. I WISH THEY WOULD LET ME DO IT AT SCHOOL.
WHY DON'T YOU SHOW ME HOW TO BUILD SOMETHING WITH THESE?
SOON...
I'M USING TRIANGLES TO MAKE PEAKS AND THE CYLINDERS TO MAKE COLUMNS. THE BRIDGES ARE RECTANGULAR. I'M GOING TO MAKE IT TALL—
I'M DONE WITH THE BLOCKS. LET'S PLAY WITH THIS.
NO! STOP IT! YOU'RE RUINING IT!
THAT'S ENOUGH FOR TODAY. LET'S GET YOUR PARENTS NOW.

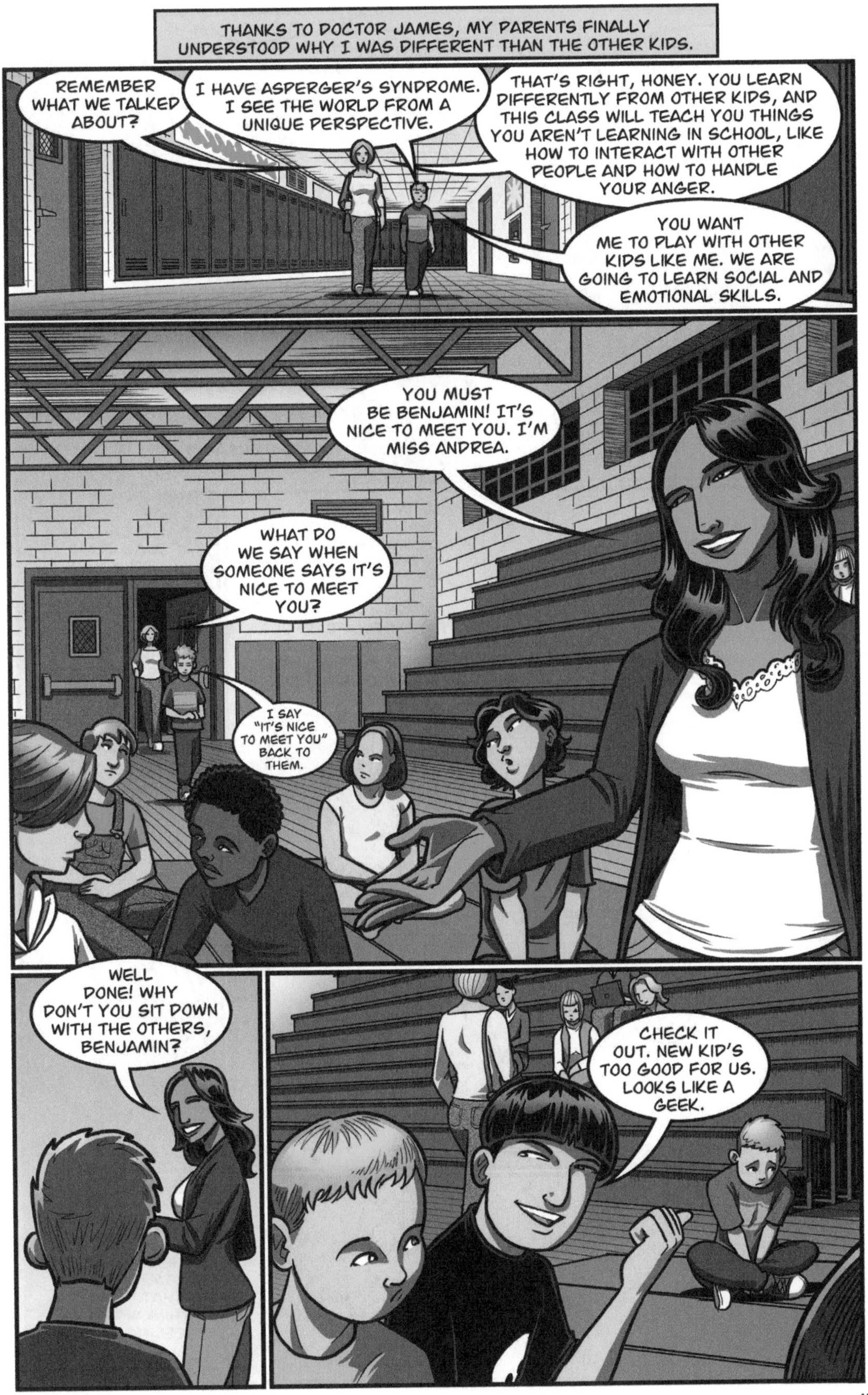
THANKS TO DOCTOR JAMES, MY PARENTS FINALLY UNDERSTOOD WHY I WAS DIFFERENT THAN THE OTHER KIDS.
REMEMBER WHAT WE TALKED ABOUT?
I HAVE ASPERGER'S SYNDROME. I SEE THE WORLD FROM A UNIQUE PERSPECTIVE.
THAT'S RIGHT, HONEY. YOU LEARN DIFFERENTLY FROM OTHER KIDS, AND THIS CLASS WILL TEACH YOU THINGS YOU AREN'T LEARNING IN SCHOOL, LIKE HOW TO INTERACT WITH OTHER PEOPLE AND HOW TO HANDLE YOUR ANGER.
YOU WANT ME TO PLAY WITH OTHER KIDS LIKE ME. WE ARE GOING TO LEARN SOCIAL AND EMOTIONAL SKILLS.
YOU MUST BE BENJAMIN! IT'S NICE TO MEET YOU. I'M MISS ANDREA.
WHAT DO WE SAY WHEN SOMEONE SAYS IT'S NICE TO MEET YOU?
I SAY "IT'S NICE TO MEET YOU" BACK TO THEM.
WELL DONE! WHY DON'T YOU SIT DOWN WITH THE OTHERS, BENJAMIN?
CHECK IT OUT. NEW KID'S TOO GOOD FOR US. LOOKS LIKE A GEEK.

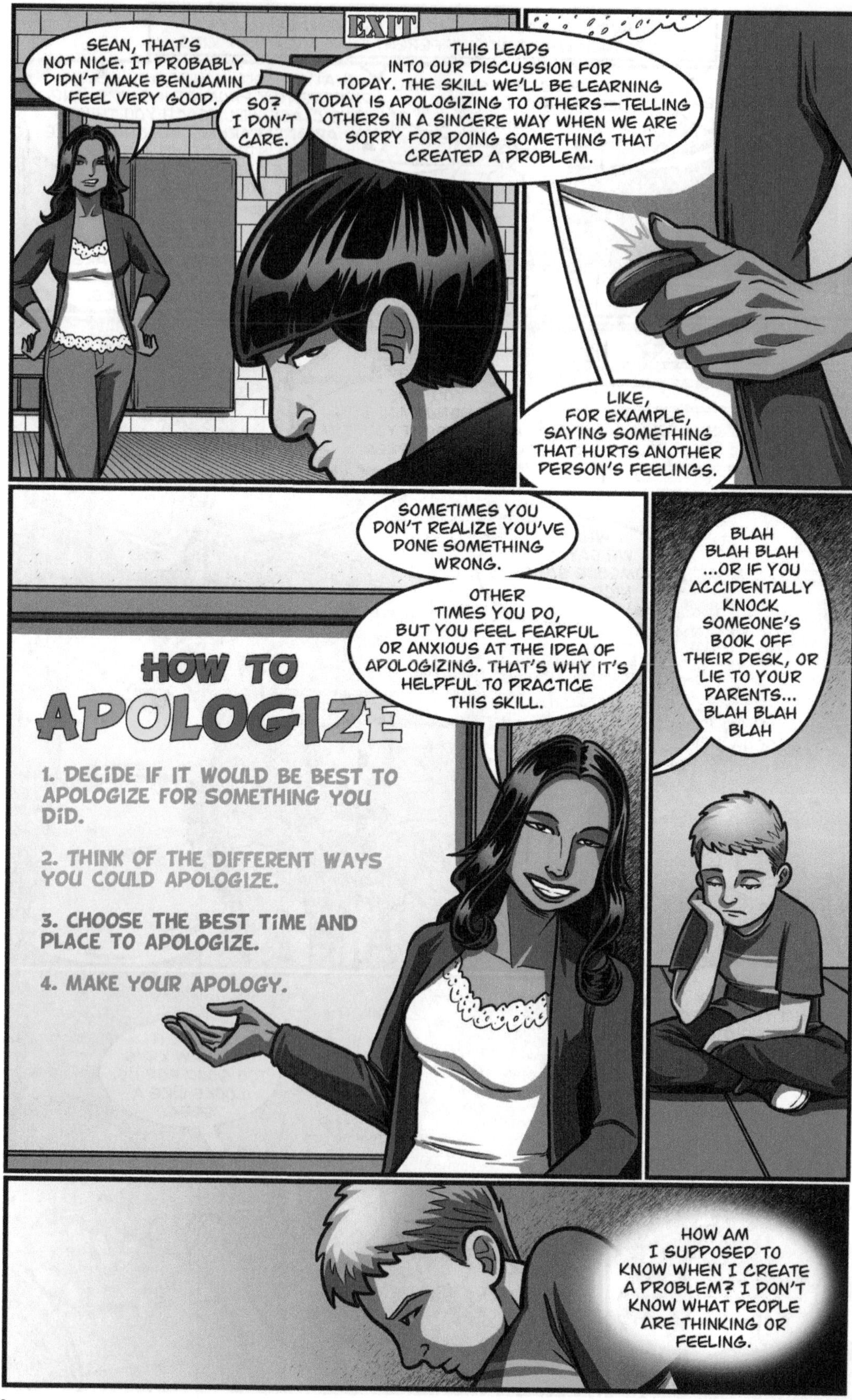
EXIT
SEAN, THAT'S NOT NICE. IT PROBABLY DIDN'T MAKE BENJAMIN FEEL VERY GOOD.
SO? I DON'T CARE.
THIS LEADS INTO OUR DISCUSSION FOR TODAY. THE SKILL WE'LL BE LEARNING TODAY IS APOLOGIZING TO OTHERS—TELLING OTHERS IN A SINCERE WAY WHEN WE ARE SORRY FOR DOING SOMETHING THAT CREATED A PROBLEM.
LIKE, FOR EXAMPLE, SAYING SOMETHING THAT HURTS ANOTHER PERSON'S FEELINGS.
SOMETIMES YOU DON'T REALIZE YOU'VE DONE SOMETHING WRONG.
OTHER TIMES YOU DO, BUT YOU FEEL FEARFUL OR ANXIOUS AT THE IDEA OF APOLOGIZING. THAT'S WHY IT'S HELPFUL TO PRACTICE THIS SKILL.
HOW TO APOLOGIZE
1. DECIDE IF IT WOULD BE BEST TO APOLOGIZE FOR SOMETHING YOU DID.
2. THINK OF THE DIFFERENT WAYS YOU COULD APOLOGIZE.
3. CHOOSE THE BEST TIME AND PLACE TO APOLOGIZE.
4. MAKE YOUR APOLOGY.
BLAH BLAH BLAH ...OR IF YOU ACCIDENTALLY KNOCK SOMEONE'S BOOK OFF THEIR DESK, OR LIE TO YOUR PARENTS... BLAH BLAH BLAH
HOW AM I SUPPOSED TO KNOW WHEN I CREATE A PROBLEM? I DON'T KNOW WHAT PEOPLE ARE THINKING OR FEELING.

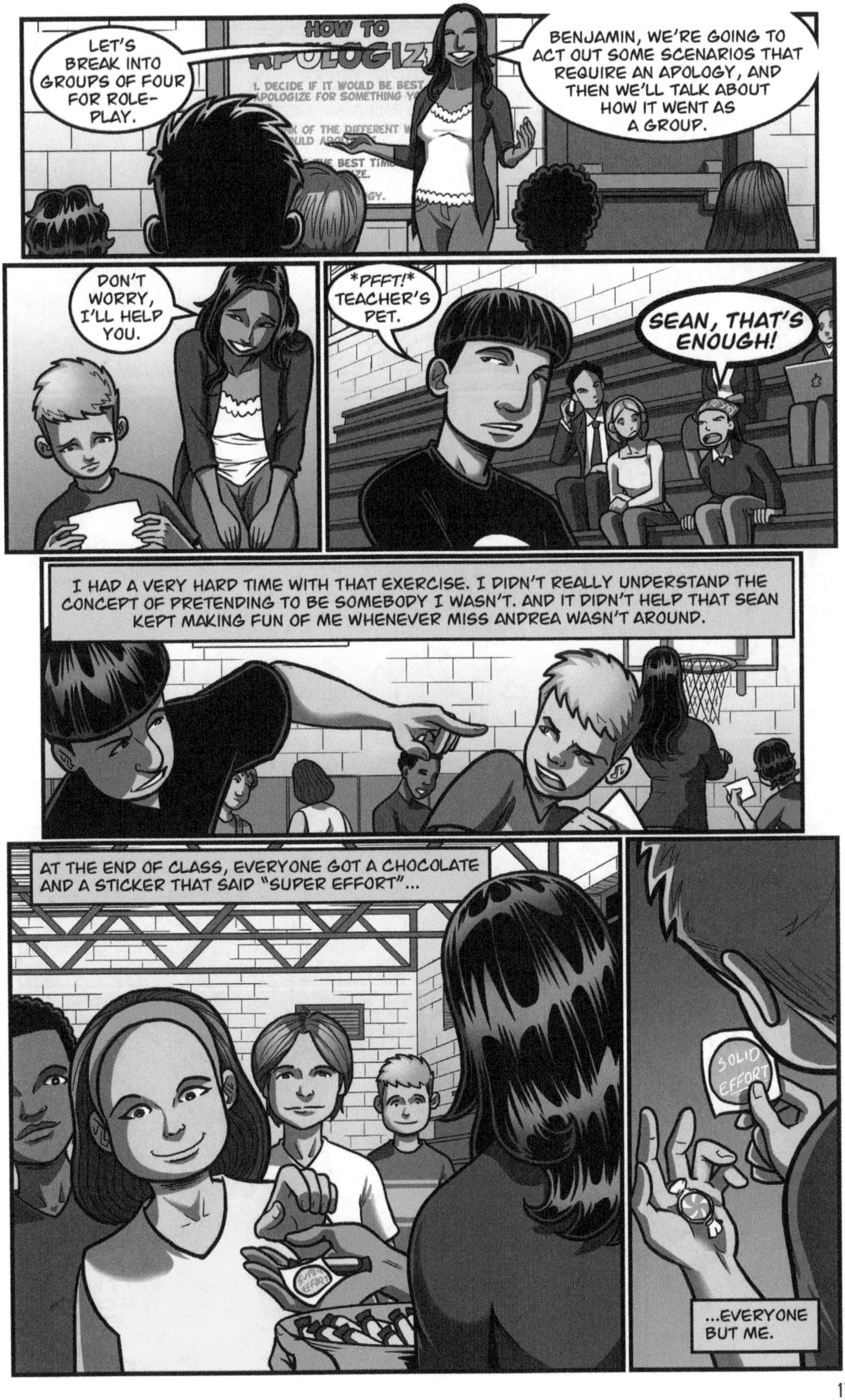
HOW TO
LET'S BREAK INTO GROUPS OF FOUR FOR ROLE-PLAY.
BENJAMIN, WE'RE GOING TO ACT OUT SOME SCENARIOS THAT REQUIRE AN APOLOGY, AND THEN WE'LL TALK ABOUT HOW IT WENT AS A GROUP.
DON'T WORRY, I'LL HELP YOU.
PFFT! TEACHER'S PET.
SEAN, THAT'S ENOUGH!
I HAD A VERY HARD TIME WITH THAT EXERCISE. I DIDN'T REALLY UNDERSTAND THE CONCEPT OF PRETENDING TO BE SOMEBODY I WASN'T. AND IT DIDN'T HELP THAT SEAN KEPT MAKING FUN OF ME WHENEVER MISS ANDREA WASN'T AROUND.
AT THE END OF CLASS, EVERYONE GOT A CHOCOLATE AND A STICKER THAT SAID "SUPER EFFORT"...
SUPER EFFORT
SOLID EFFORT
...EVERYONE BUT ME.

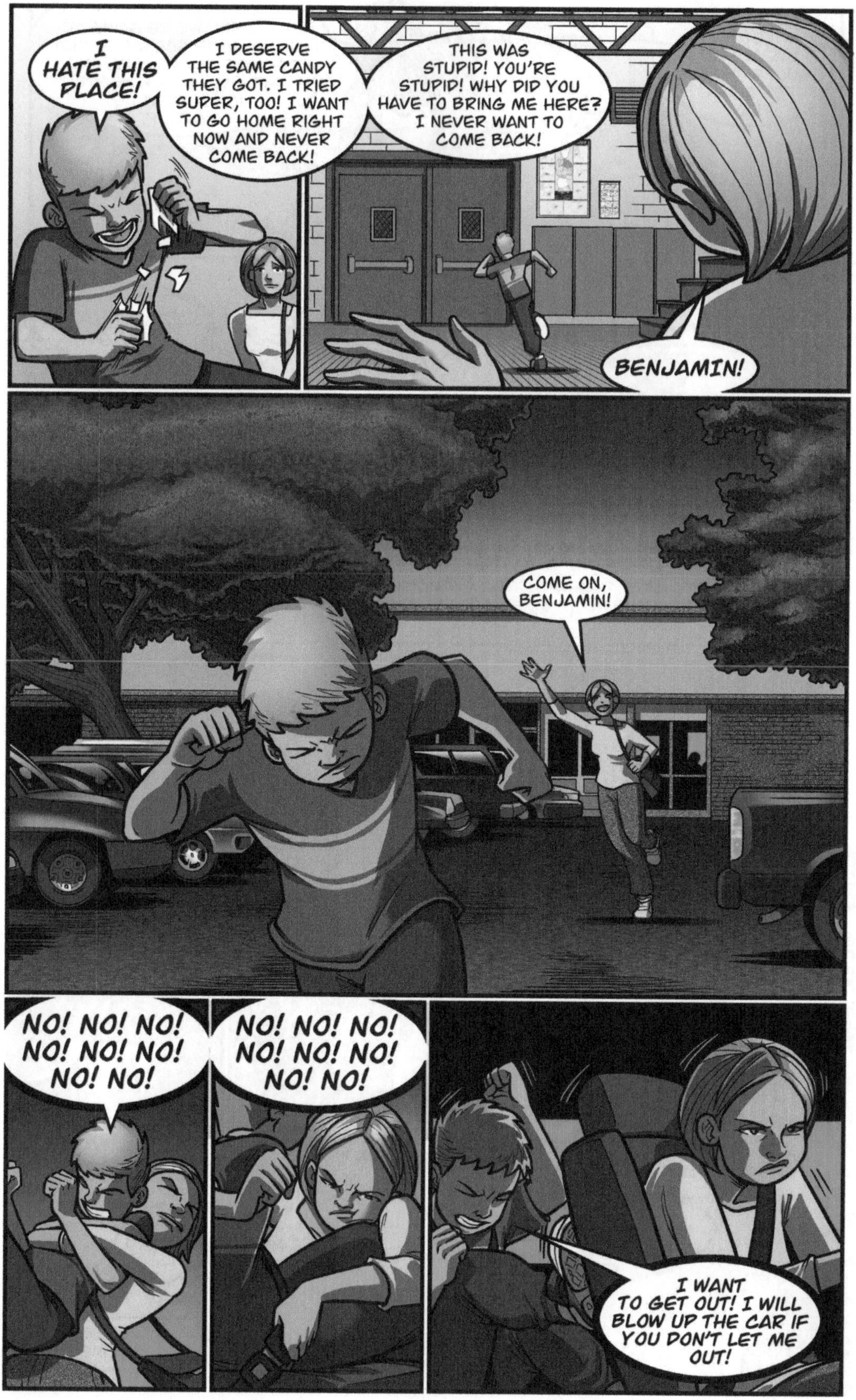
I HATE THIS PLACE!
I DESERVE THE SAME CANDY THEY GOT. I TRIED SUPER, TOO! I WANT TO GO HOME RIGHT NOW AND NEVER COME BACK!
THIS WAS STUPID! YOU'RE STUPID! WHY DID YOU HAVE TO BRING ME HERE? I NEVER WANT TO COME BACK!
BENJAMIN!
COME ON, BENJAMIN!
NO! NO! NO! NO! NO! NO! NO! NO!
NO! NO! NO! NO! NO! NO! NO! NO!
I WANT TO GET OUT! I WILL BLOW UP THE CAR IF YOU DON'T LET ME OUT!

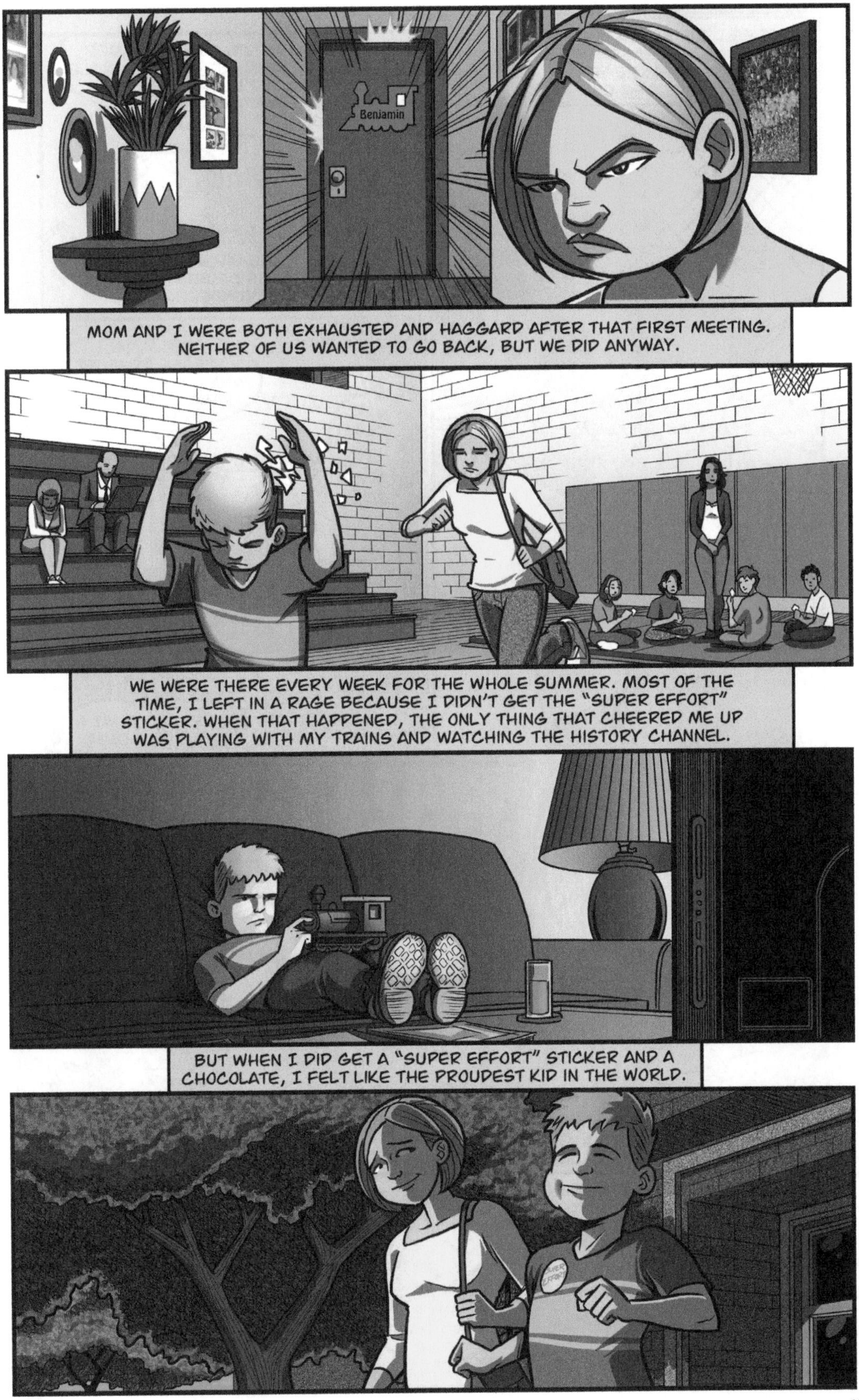
Benjamin
MOM AND I WERE BOTH EXHAUSTED AND HAGGARD AFTER THAT FIRST MEETING. NEITHER OF US WANTED TO GO BACK, BUT WE DID ANYWAY.
WE WERE THERE EVERY WEEK FOR THE WHOLE SUMMER. MOST OF THE TIME, I LEFT IN A RAGE BECAUSE I DIDN'T GET THE "SUPER EFFORT" STICKER. WHEN THAT HAPPENED, THE ONLY THING THAT CHEERED ME UP WAS PLAYING WITH MY TRAINS AND WATCHING THE HISTORY CHANNEL.
BUT WHEN I DID GET A "SUPER EFFORT" STICKER AND A CHOCOLATE, I FELT LIKE THE PROUDEST KID IN THE WORLD.

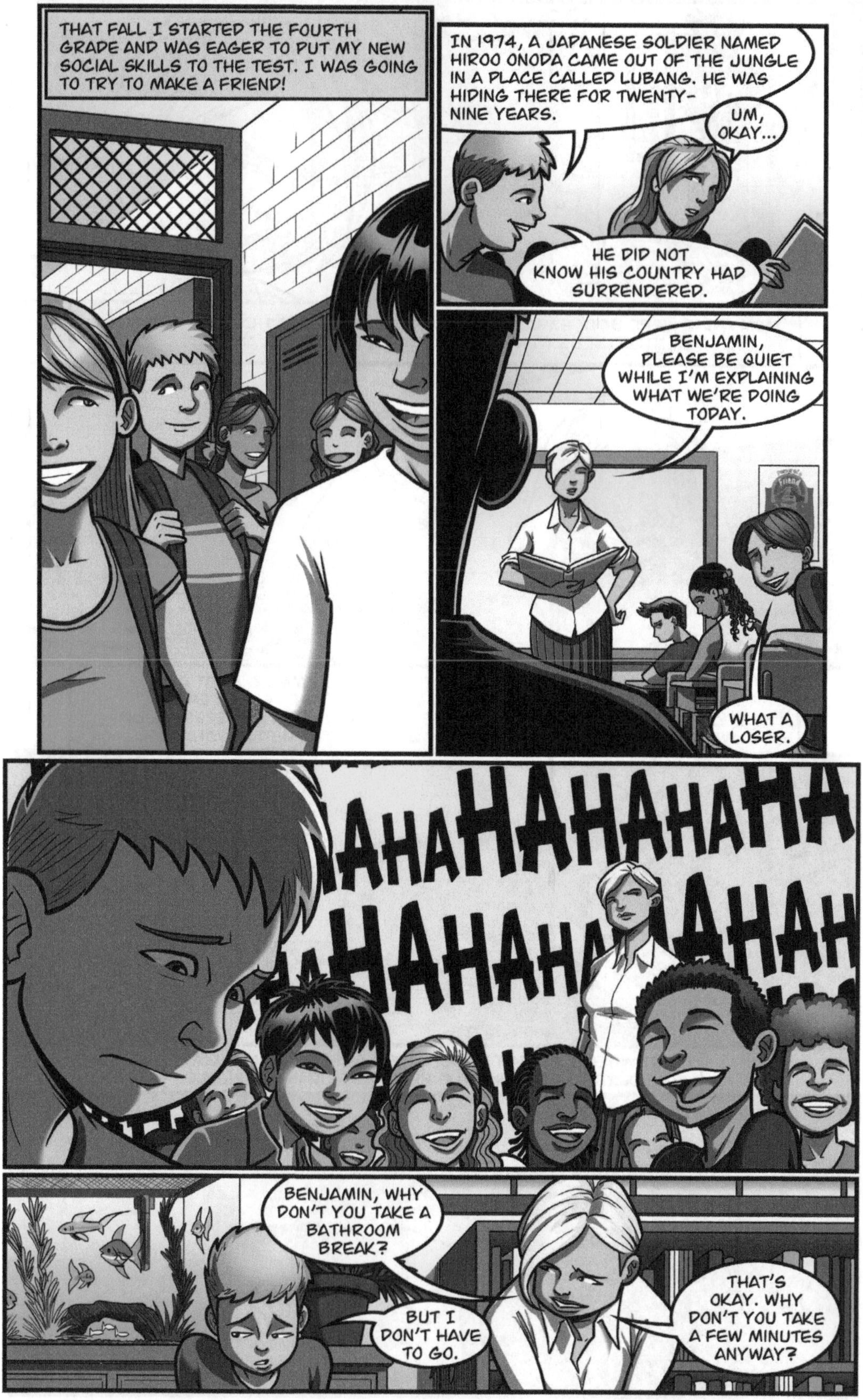

THAT FALL I STARTED THE FOURTH GRADE AND WAS EAGER TO PUT MY NEW SOCIAL SKILLS TO THE TEST. I WAS GOING TO TRY TO MAKE A FRIEND!
IN 1974, A JAPANESE SOLDIER NAMED HIROO ONODA CAME OUT OF THE JUNGLE IN A PLACE CALLED LUBANG. HE WAS HIDING THERE FOR TWENTY-NINE YEARS.
UM, OKAY...
HE DID NOT KNOW HIS COUNTRY HAD SURRENDERED.
BENJAMIN, PLEASE BE QUIET WHILE I'M EXPLAINING WHAT WE'RE DOING TODAY.
WHAT A LOSER.
HAHAHAHAHAHAHA
BENJAMIN, WHY DON'T YOU TAKE A BATHROOM BREAK?
BUT I DON'T HAVE TO GO.
THAT'S OKAY. WHY DON'T YOU TAKE A FEW MINUTES ANYWAY?

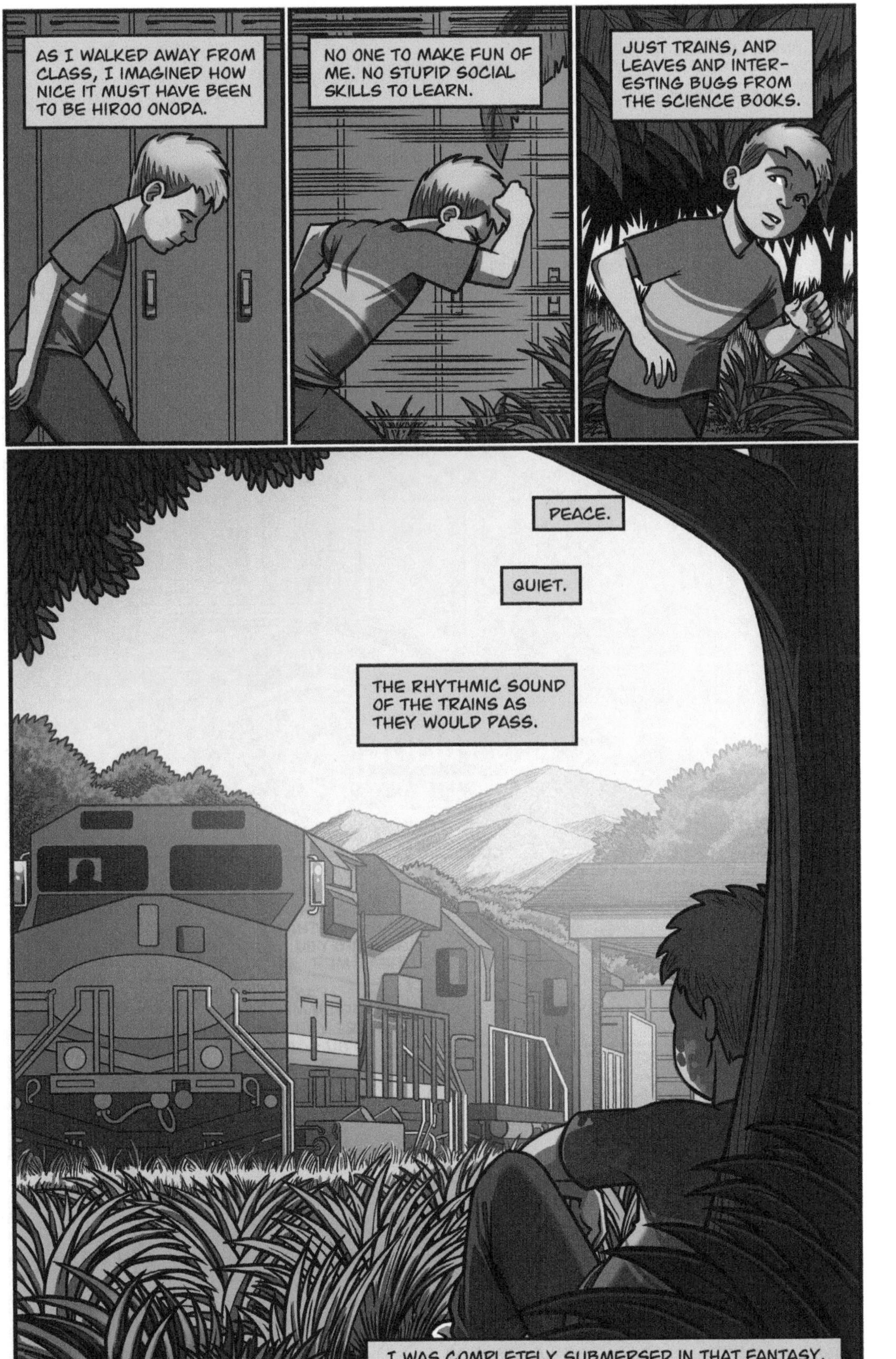
AS I WALKED AWAY FROM CLASS, I IMAGINED HOW NICE IT MUST HAVE BEEN TO BE HIROO ONODA.
NO ONE TO MAKE FUN OF ME. NO STUPID SOCIAL SKILLS TO LEARN.
JUST TRAINS, AND LEAVES AND INTERESTING BUGS FROM THE SCIENCE BOOKS.
PEACE.
QUIET.
THE RHYTHMIC SOUND OF THE TRAINS AS THEY WOULD PASS.
I WAS COMPLETELY SUBMERSED IN THAT FANTASY.

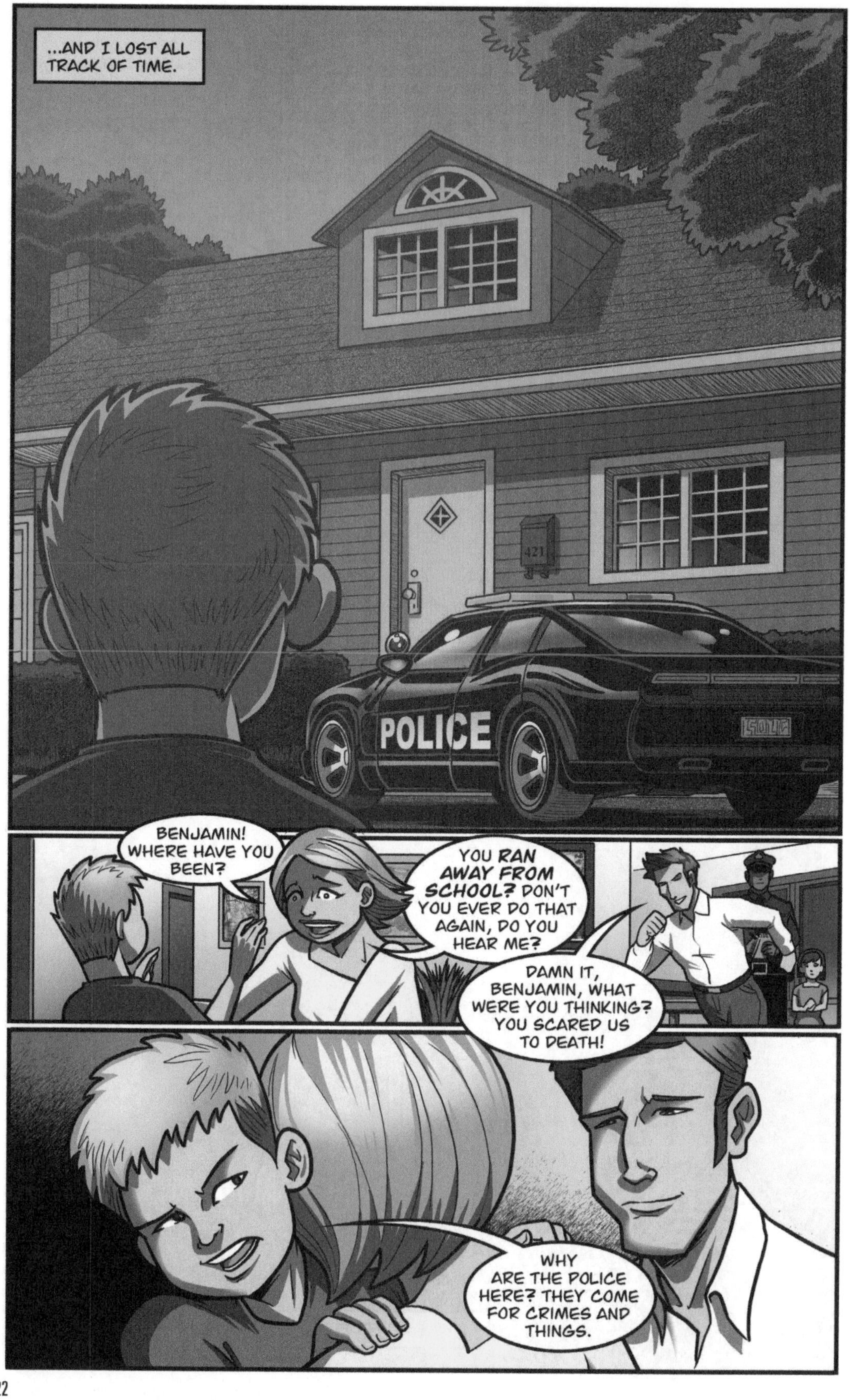

...AND I LOST ALL TRACK OF TIME.
POLICE
BENJAMIN! WHERE HAVE YOU BEEN?
YOU RAN AWAY FROM SCHOOL? DON'T YOU EVER DO THAT AGAIN, DO YOU HEAR ME?
DAMN IT, BENJAMIN, WHAT WERE YOU THINKING? YOU SCARED US TO DEATH!
WHY ARE THE POLICE HERE? THEY COME FOR CRIMES AND THINGS.

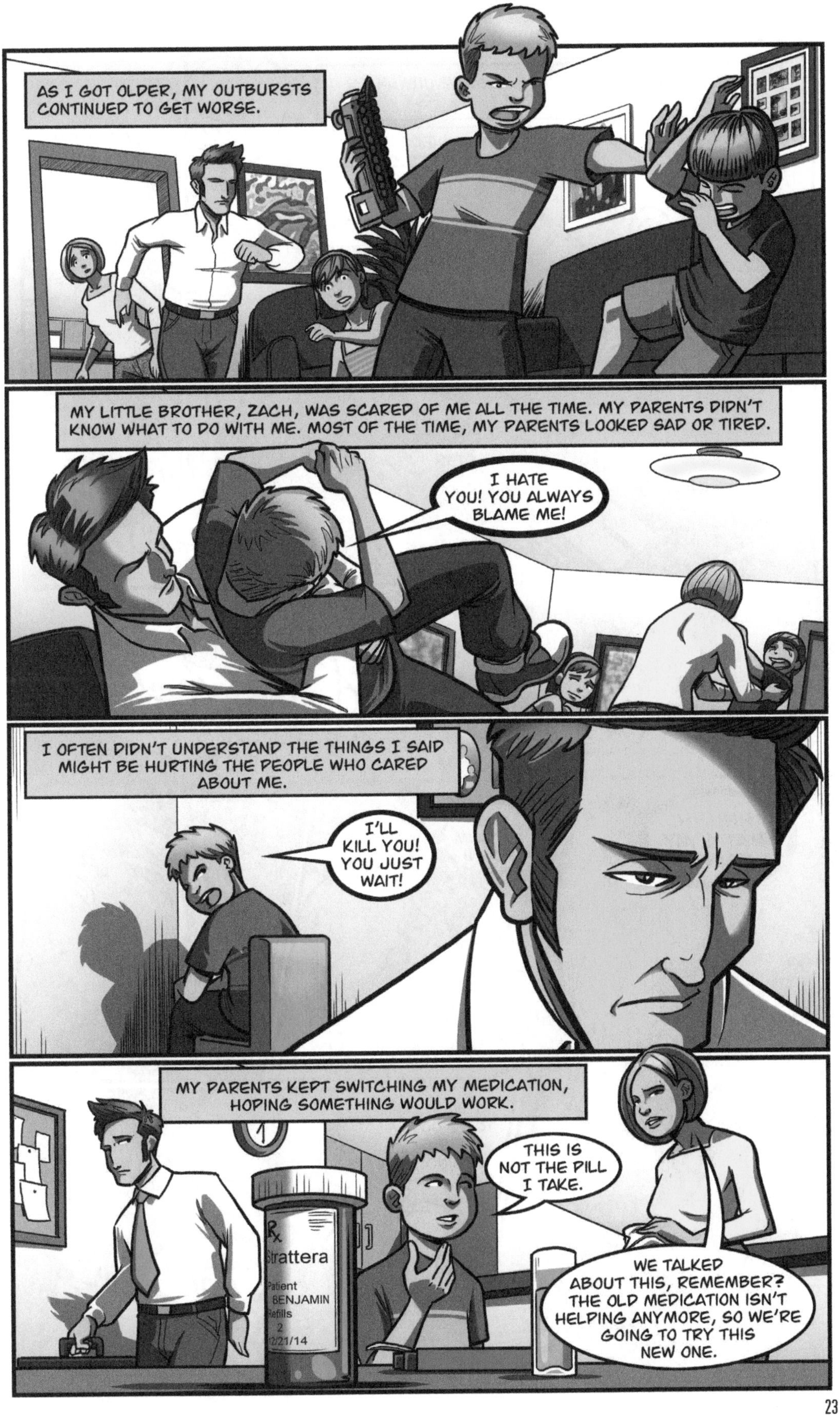
AS I GOT OLDER, MY OUTBURSTS CONTINUED TO GET WORSE.
MY LITTLE BROTHER, ZACH, WAS SCARED OF ME ALL THE TIME. MY PARENTS DIDN'T KNOW WHAT TO DO WITH ME. MOST OF THE TIME, MY PARENTS LOOKED SAD OR TIRED.
I HATE YOU! YOU ALWAYS BLAME ME!
I OFTEN DIDN'T UNDERSTAND THE THINGS I SAID MIGHT BE HURTING THE PEOPLE WHO CARED ABOUT ME.
I'LL KILL YOU! YOU JUST WAIT!
MY PARENTS KEPT SWITCHING MY MEDICATION, HOPING SOMETHING WOULD WORK.
THIS IS NOT THE PILL I TAKE.
Rx
Strattera
Patient
BENJAMIN
Refills
2
12/21/14
WE TALKED ABOUT THIS, REMEMBER? THE OLD MEDICATION ISN'T HELPING ANYMORE, SO WE'RE GOING TO TRY THIS NEW ONE.

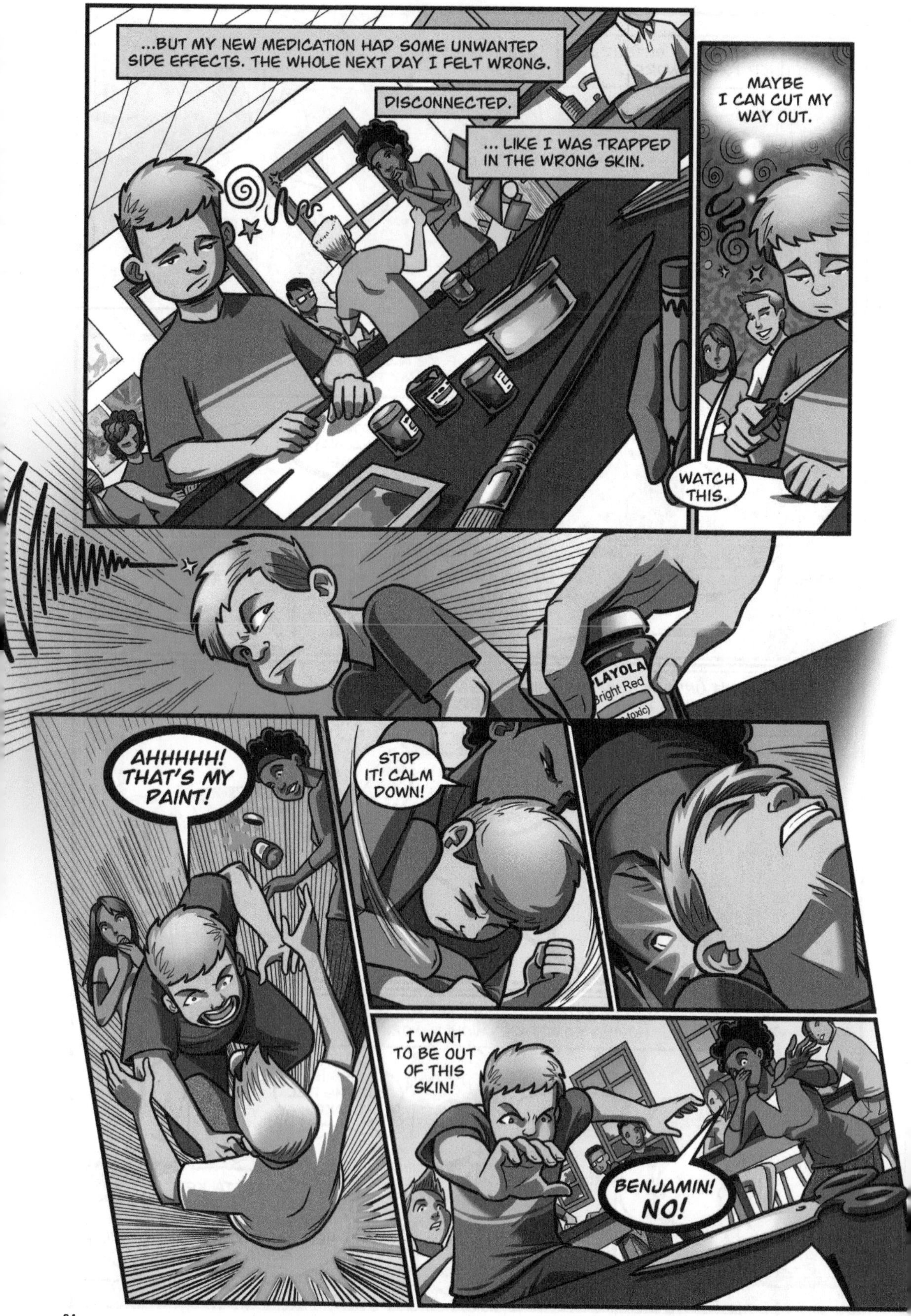
...BUT MY NEW MEDICATION HAD SOME UNWANTED SIDE EFFECTS. THE WHOLE NEXT DAY I FELT WRONG.
DISCONNECTED.
... LIKE I WAS TRAPPED IN THE WRONG SKIN.
MAYBE I CAN CUT MY WAY OUT.
WATCH THIS.
LAYOLA
Bright Red
AHHHHH! THAT'S MY PAINT!
STOP IT! CALM DOWN!
I WANT TO BE OUT OF THIS SKIN!
BENJAMIN! NO!

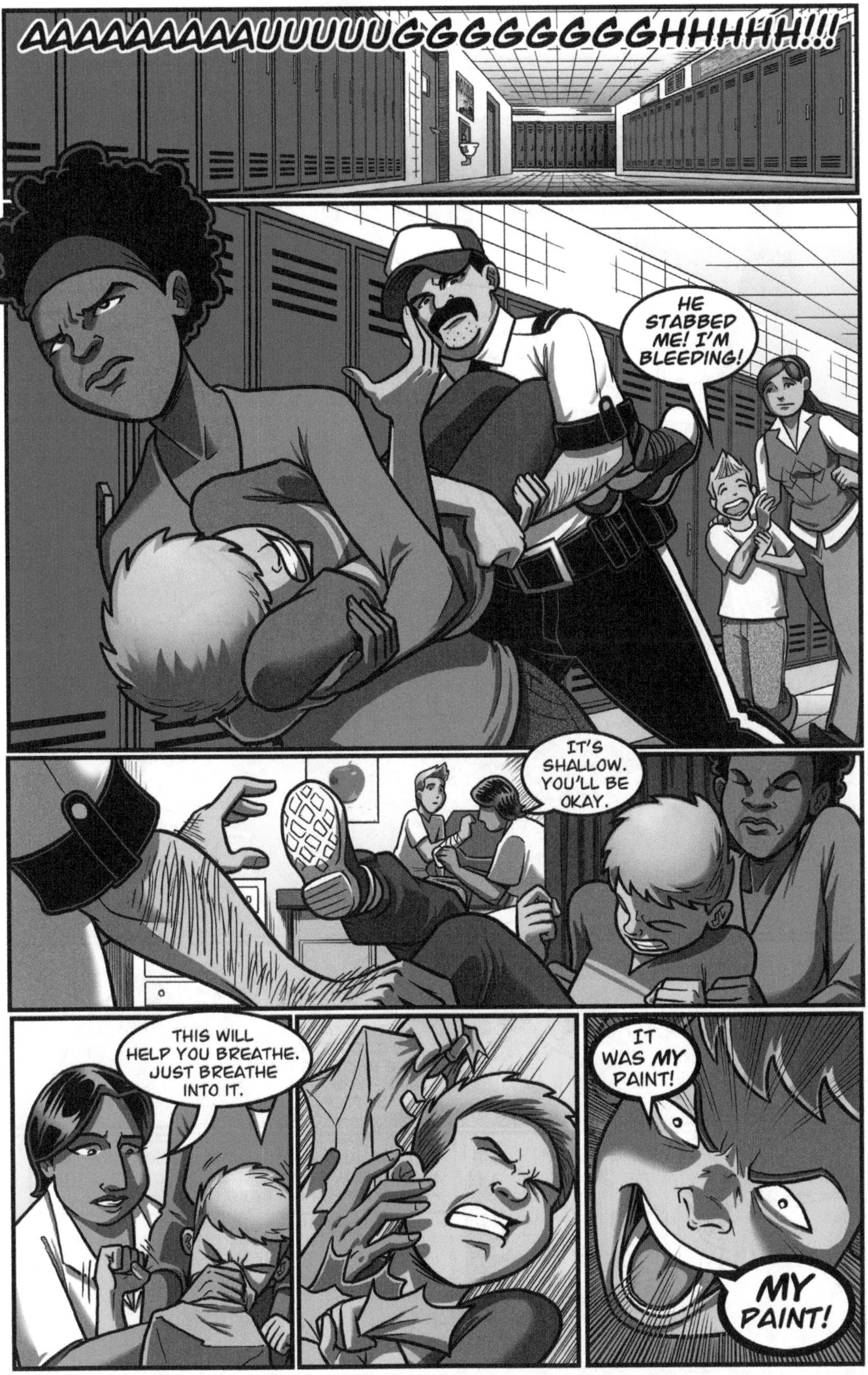
AAAAAAAAAUUUUUGGGGGGGGHHHHH!!!
HE STABBED ME! I'M BLEEDING!
IT'S SHALLOW. YOU'LL BE OKAY.
THIS WILL HELP YOU BREATHE. JUST BREATHE INTO IT.
IT WAS MY PAINT!
MY PAINT!

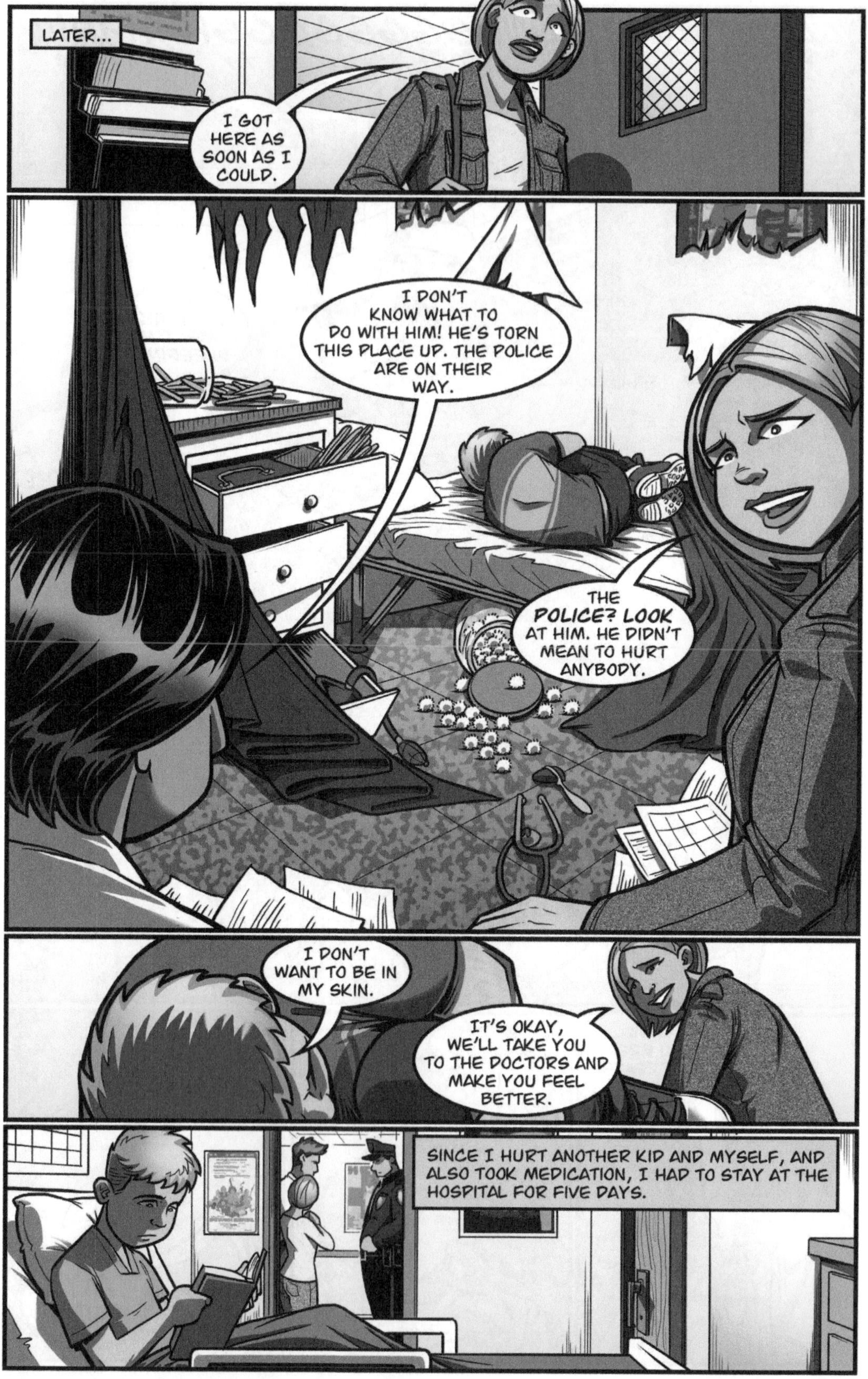
LATER...
I GOT HERE AS SOON AS I COULD.
I DON'T KNOW WHAT TO DO WITH HIM! HE'S TORN THIS PLACE UP. THE POLICE ARE ON THEIR WAY.
THE POLICE? LOOK AT HIM. HE DIDN'T MEAN TO HURT ANYBODY.
I DON'T WANT TO BE IN MY SKIN.
IT'S OKAY, WE'LL TAKE YOU TO THE DOCTORS AND MAKE YOU FEEL BETTER.
SINCE I HURT ANOTHER KID AND MYSELF, AND ALSO TOOK MEDICATION, I HAD TO STAY AT THE HOSPITAL FOR FIVE DAYS.

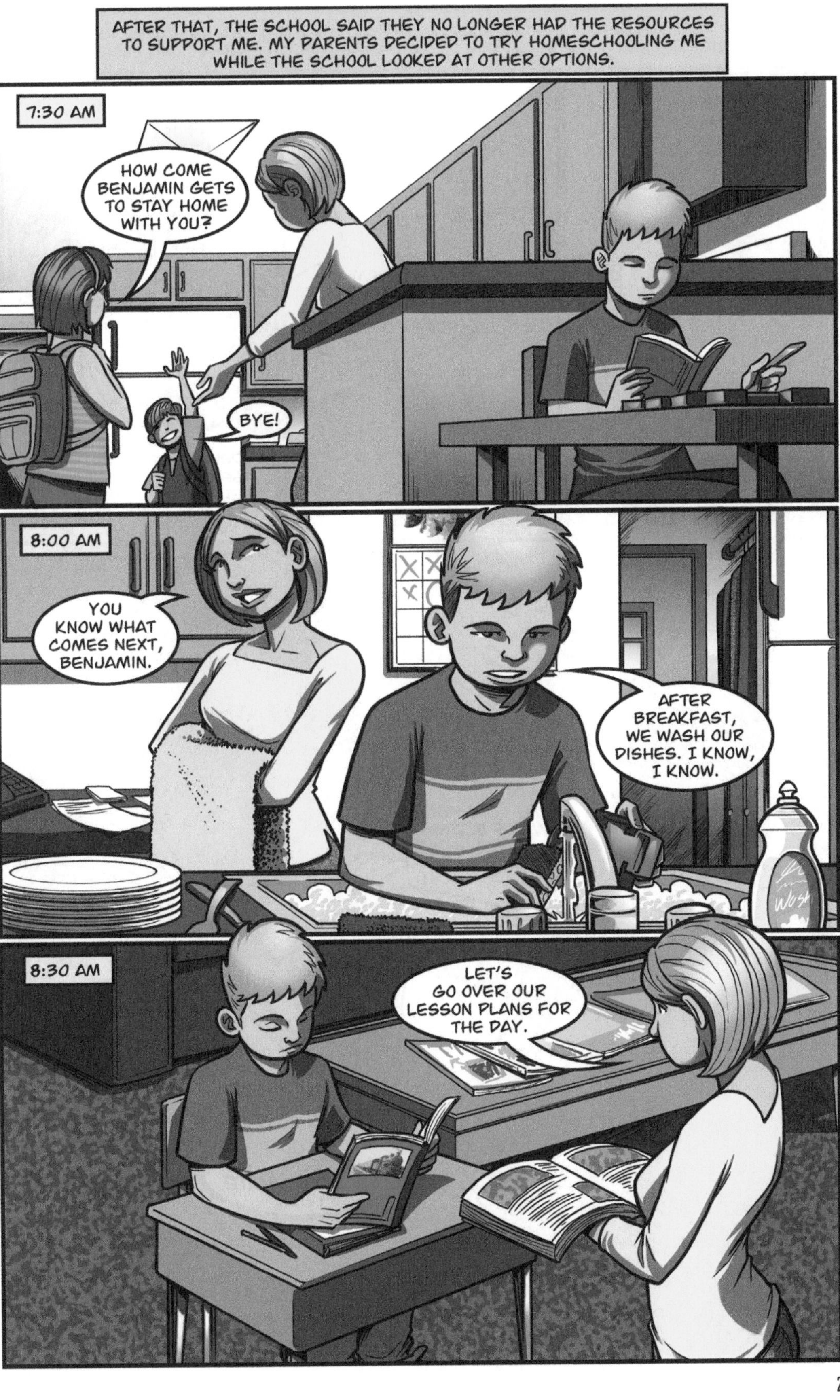
AFTER THAT, THE SCHOOL SAID THEY NO LONGER HAD THE RESOURCES TO SUPPORT ME. MY PARENTS DECIDED TO TRY HOMESCHOOLING ME WHILE THE SCHOOL LOOKED AT OTHER OPTIONS.
7:30 AM
HOW COME BENJAMIN GETS TO STAY HOME WITH YOU?
BYE!
8:00 AM
YOU KNOW WHAT COMES NEXT, BENJAMIN.
AFTER BREAKFAST, WE WASH OUR DISHES. I KNOW, I KNOW.
8:30 AM
LET'S GO OVER OUR LESSON PLANS FOR THE DAY.

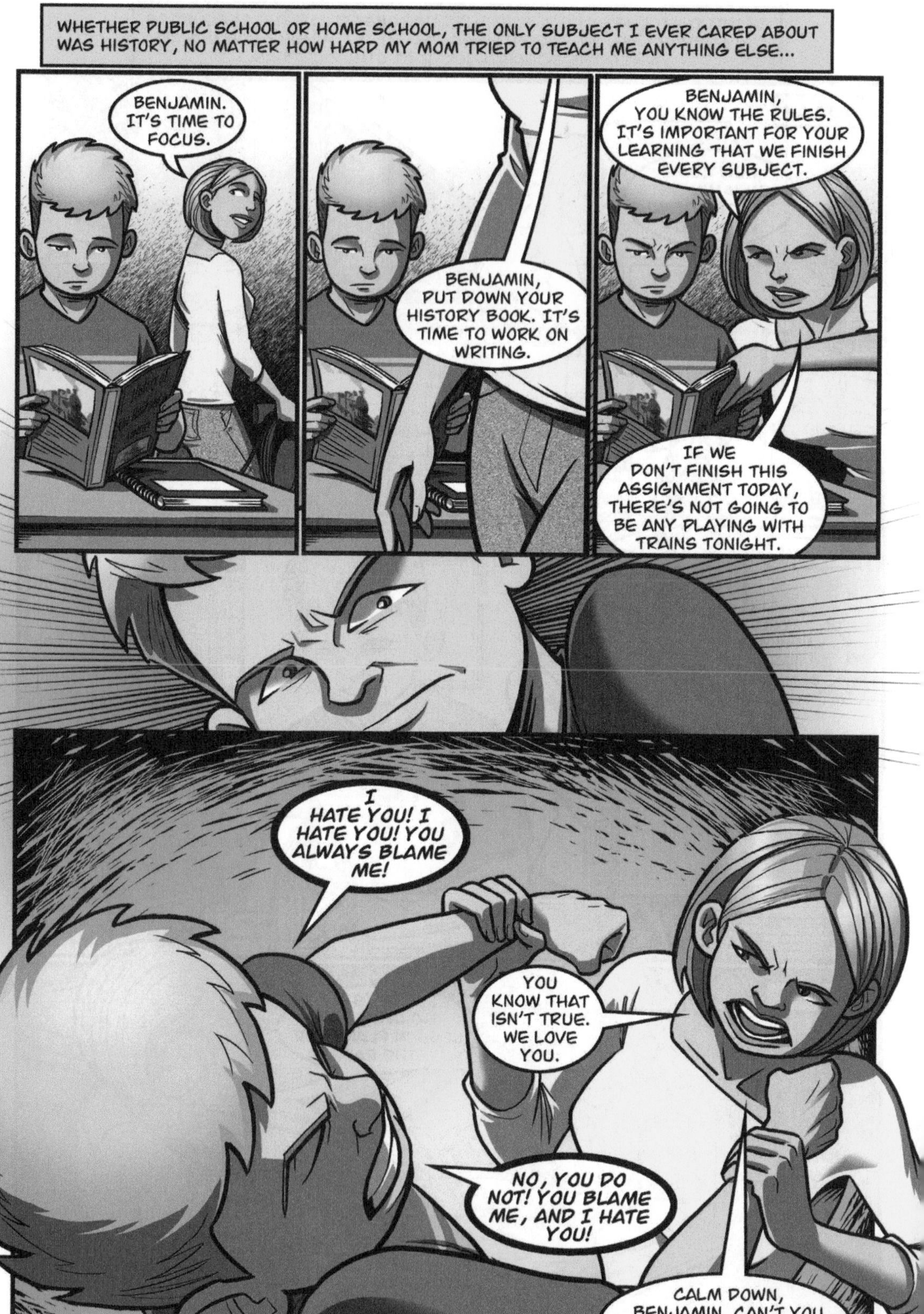
WHETHER PUBLIC SCHOOL OR HOME SCHOOL, THE ONLY SUBJECT I EVER CARED ABOUT WAS HISTORY, NO MATTER HOW HARD MY MOM TRIED TO TEACH ME ANYTHING ELSE...
BENJAMIN. IT'S TIME TO FOCUS.
BENJAMIN, PUT DOWN YOUR HISTORY BOOK. IT'S TIME TO WORK ON WRITING.
BENJAMIN, YOU KNOW THE RULES. IT'S IMPORTANT FOR YOUR LEARNING THAT WE FINISH EVERY SUBJECT.
IF WE DON'T FINISH THIS ASSIGNMENT TODAY, THERE'S NOT GOING TO BE ANY PLAYING WITH TRAINS TONIGHT.
I HATE YOU! I HATE YOU! YOU ALWAYS BLAME ME!
YOU KNOW THAT ISN'T TRUE. WE LOVE YOU.
NO, YOU DO NOT! YOU BLAME ME, AND I HATE YOU!
CALM DOWN, BENJAMIN. CAN'T YOU SEE THAT YOU'RE ACTING UNREASONABLY?

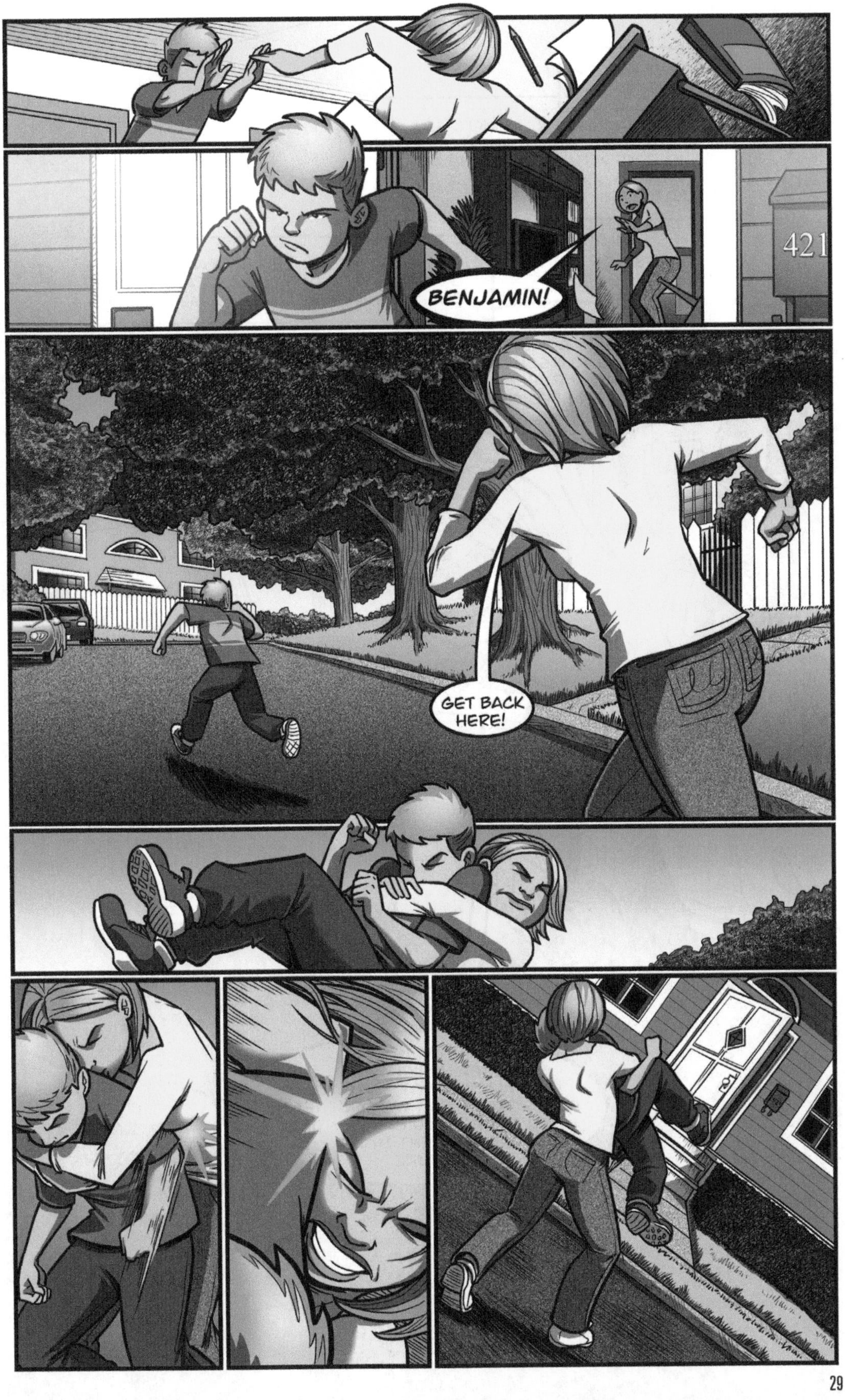
421
BENJAMIN!
GET BACK HERE!

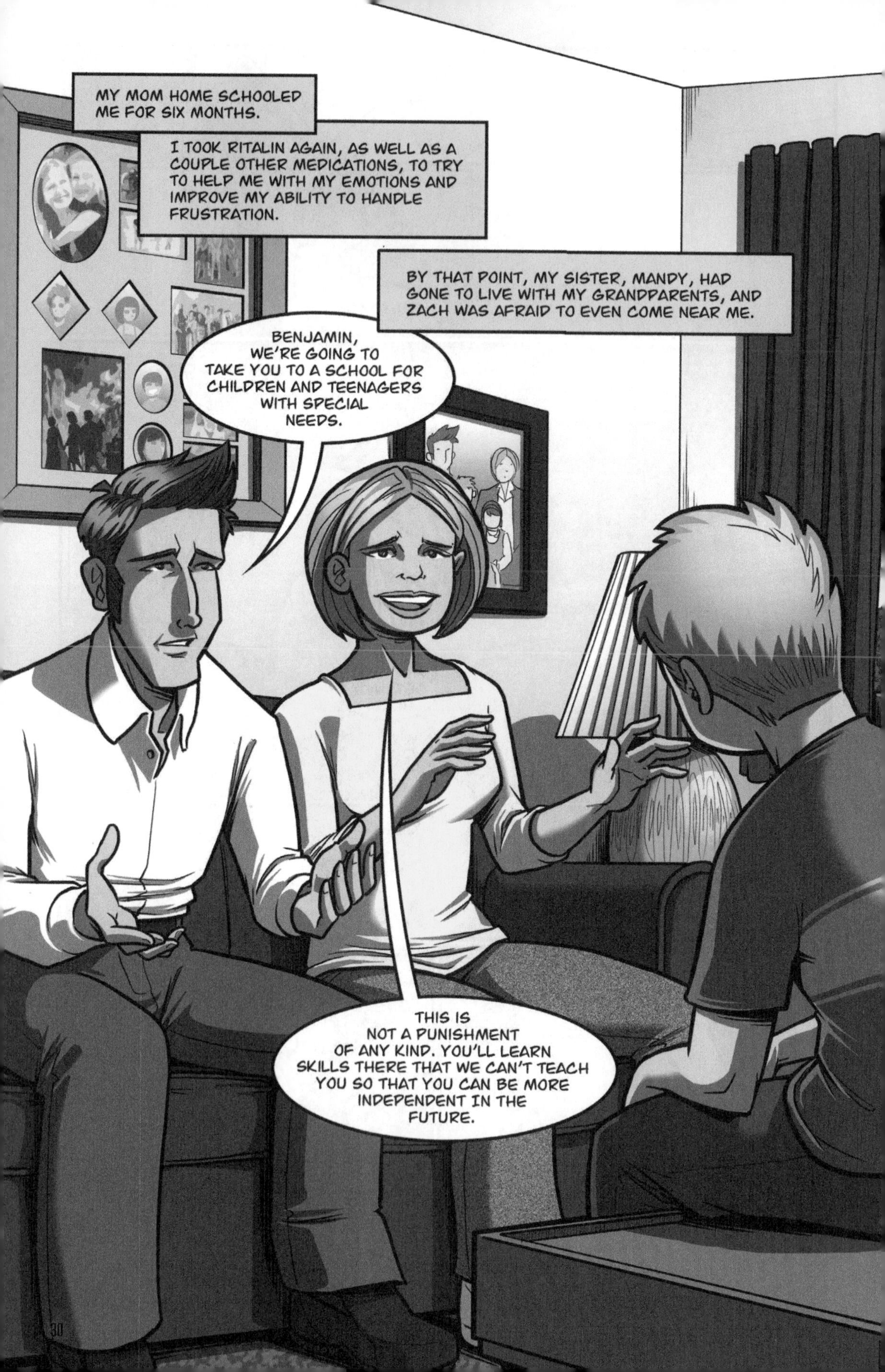
MY MOM HOME SCHOOLED ME FOR SIX MONTHS.
I TOOK RITALIN AGAIN, AS WELL AS A COUPLE OTHER MEDICATIONS, TO TRY TO HELP ME WITH MY EMOTIONS AND IMPROVE MY ABILITY TO HANDLE FRUSTRATION.
BY THAT POINT, MY SISTER, MANDY, HAD GONE TO LIVE WITH MY GRANDPARENTS, AND ZACH WAS AFRAID TO EVEN COME NEAR ME.
BENJAMIN, WE'RE GOING TO TAKE YOU TO A SCHOOL FOR CHILDREN AND TEENAGERS WITH SPECIAL NEEDS.
THIS IS NOT A PUNISHMENT OF ANY KIND. YOU'LL LEARN SKILLS THERE THAT WE CAN'T TEACH YOU SO THAT YOU CAN BE MORE INDEPENDENT IN THE FUTURE.

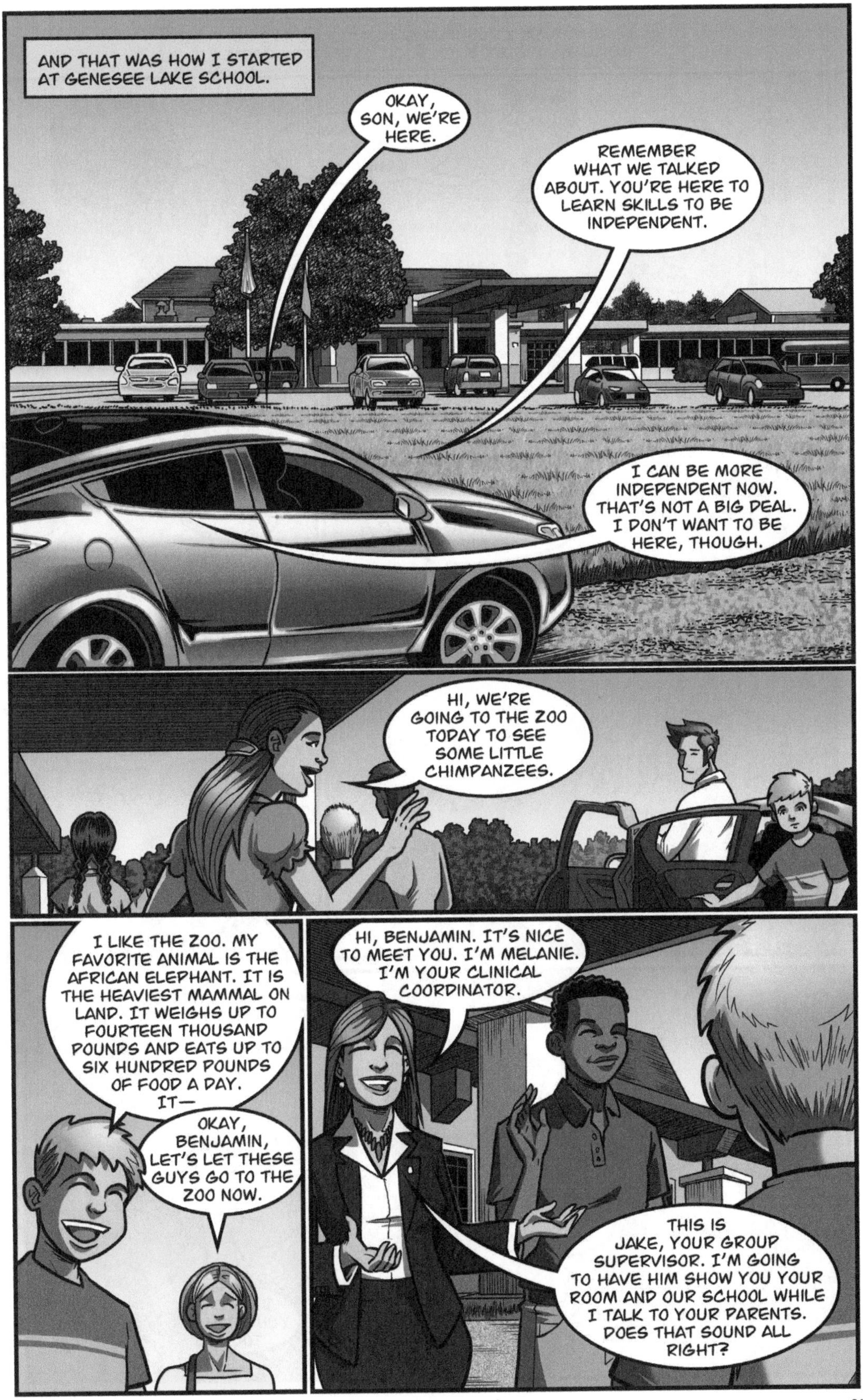
AND THAT WAS HOW I STARTED AT GENESEE LAKE SCHOOL.
OKAY, SON, WE'RE HERE.
REMEMBER WHAT WE TALKED ABOUT. YOU'RE HERE TO LEARN SKILLS TO BE INDEPENDENT.
I CAN BE MORE INDEPENDENT NOW. THAT'S NOT A BIG DEAL. I DON'T WANT TO BE HERE, THOUGH.
HI, WE'RE GOING TO THE ZOO TODAY TO SEE SOME LITTLE CHIMPANZEES.
I LIKE THE ZOO. MY FAVORITE ANIMAL IS THE AFRICAN ELEPHANT. IT IS THE HEAVIEST MAMMAL ON LAND. IT WEIGHS UP TO FOURTEEN THOUSAND POUNDS AND EATS UP TO SIX HUNDRED POUNDS OF FOOD A DAY. IT—
OKAY, BENJAMIN, LET'S LET THESE GUYS GO TO THE ZOO NOW.
HI, BENJAMIN. IT'S NICE TO MEET YOU. I'M MELANIE. I'M YOUR CLINICAL COORDINATOR.
THIS IS JAKE, YOUR GROUP SUPERVISOR. I'M GOING TO HAVE HIM SHOW YOU YOUR ROOM AND OUR SCHOOL WHILE I TALK TO YOUR PARENTS. DOES THAT SOUND ALL RIGHT?

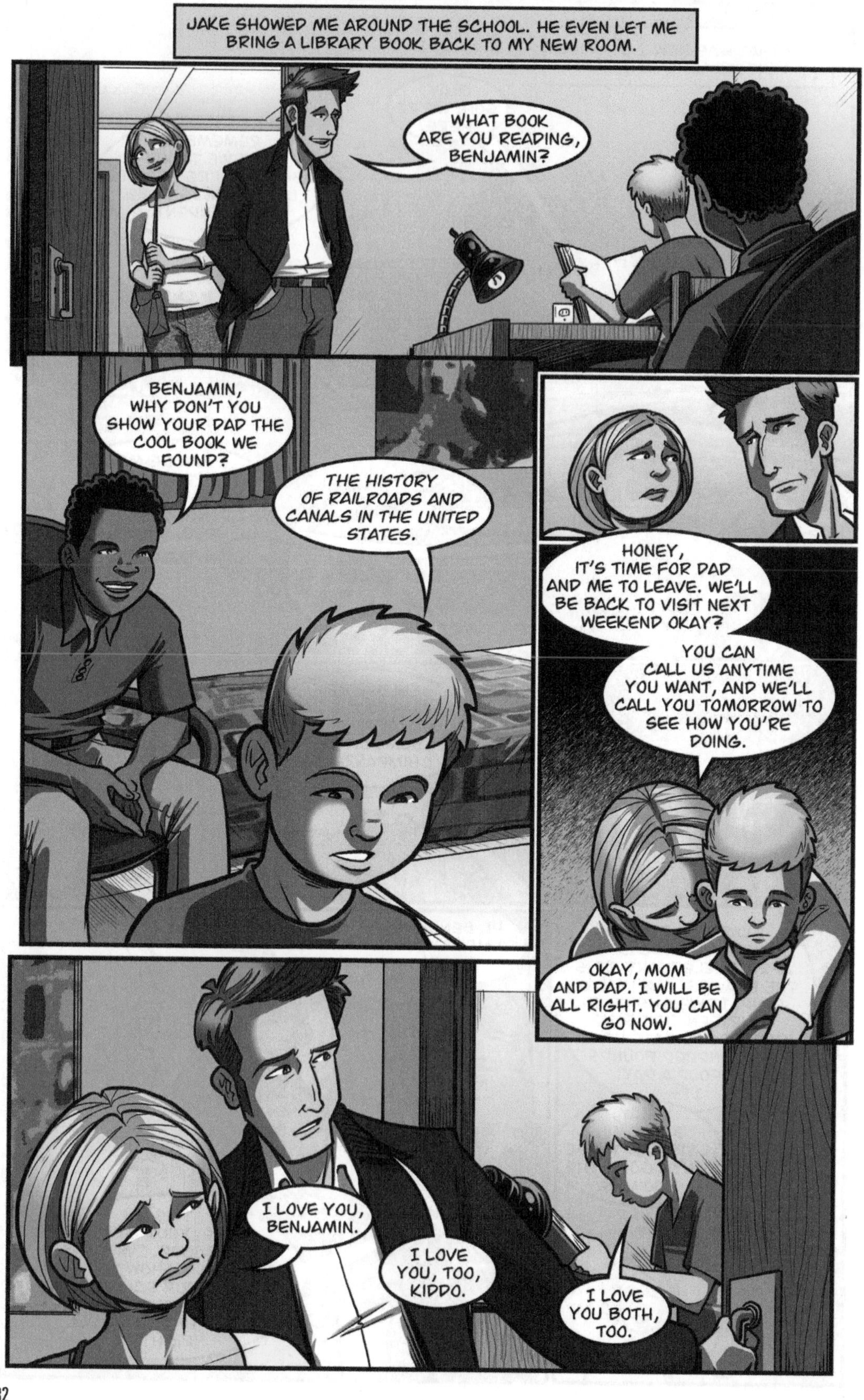
JAKE SHOWED ME AROUND THE SCHOOL. HE EVEN LET ME BRING A LIBRARY BOOK BACK TO MY NEW ROOM.
WHAT BOOK ARE YOU READING, BENJAMIN?
BENJAMIN, WHY DON'T YOU SHOW YOUR DAD THE COOL BOOK WE FOUND?
THE HISTORY OF RAILROADS AND CANALS IN THE UNITED STATES.
HONEY, IT'S TIME FOR DAD AND ME TO LEAVE. WE'LL BE BACK TO VISIT NEXT WEEKEND OKAY?
YOU CAN CALL US ANYTIME YOU WANT, AND WE'LL CALL YOU TOMORROW TO SEE HOW YOU'RE DOING.
OKAY, MOM AND DAD. I WILL BE ALL RIGHT. YOU CAN GO NOW.
I LOVE YOU, BENJAMIN.
I LOVE YOU, TOO, KIDDO.
I LOVE YOU BOTH, TOO.

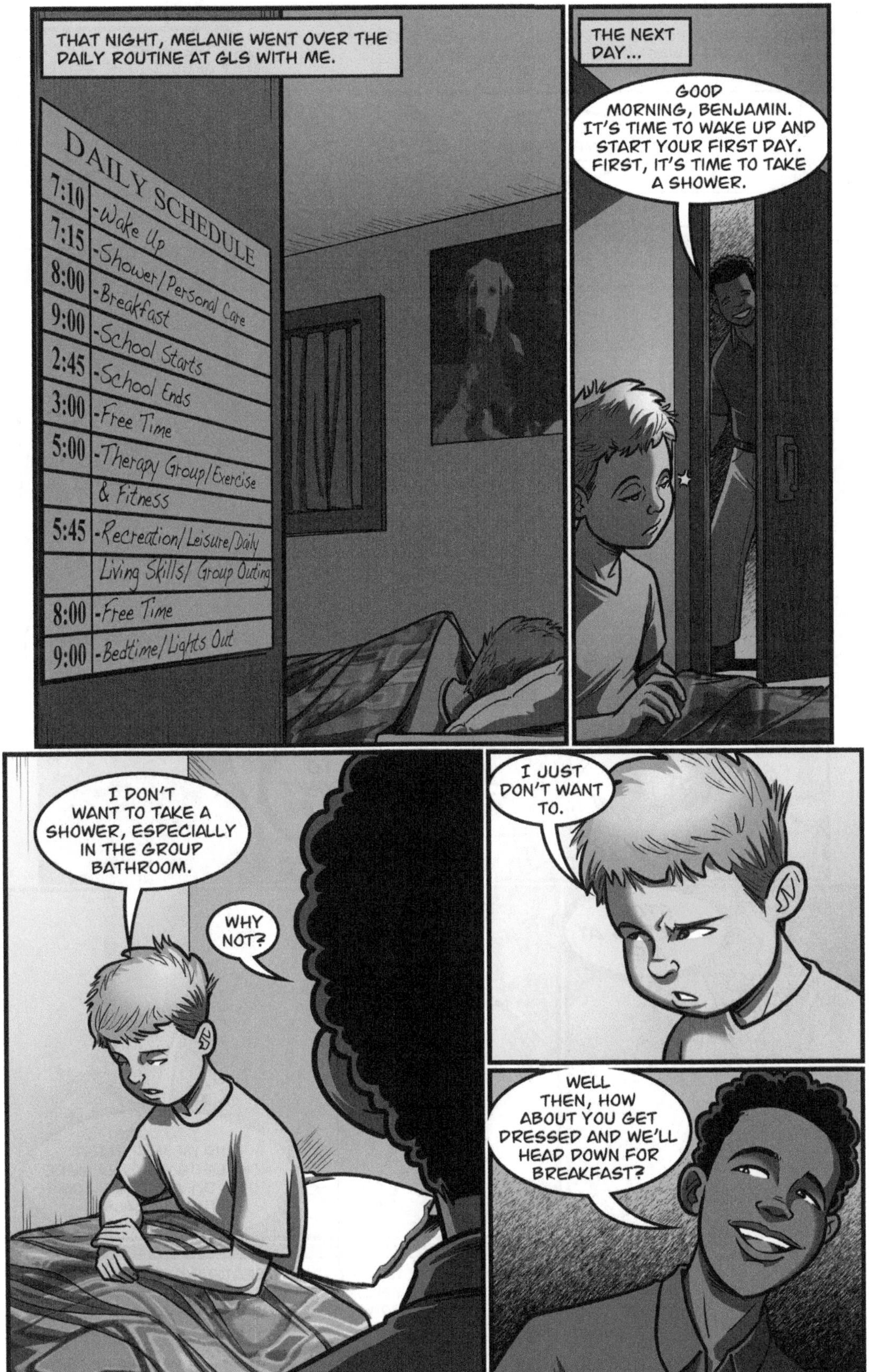
THAT NIGHT, MELANIE WENT OVER THE DAILY ROUTINE AT GLS WITH ME.
DAILY SCHEDULE
7:10 -Wake Up
7:15 -Shower/Personal Care
8:00 -Breakfast
9:00 -School Starts
2:45 -School Ends
3:00 -Free Time
5:00 -Therapy Group/Exercise & Fitness
5:45 -Recreation/Leisure/Daily Living Skills/Group Outing
8:00 -Free Time
9:00 -Bedtime/Lights Out
THE NEXT DAY...
GOOD MORNING, BENJAMIN. IT'S TIME TO WAKE UP AND START YOUR FIRST DAY. FIRST, IT'S TIME TO TAKE A SHOWER.
I DON'T WANT TO TAKE A SHOWER, ESPECIALLY IN THE GROUP BATHROOM.
WHY NOT?
I JUST DON'T WANT TO.
WELL THEN, HOW ABOUT YOU GET DRESSED AND WE'LL HEAD DOWN FOR BREAKFAST?

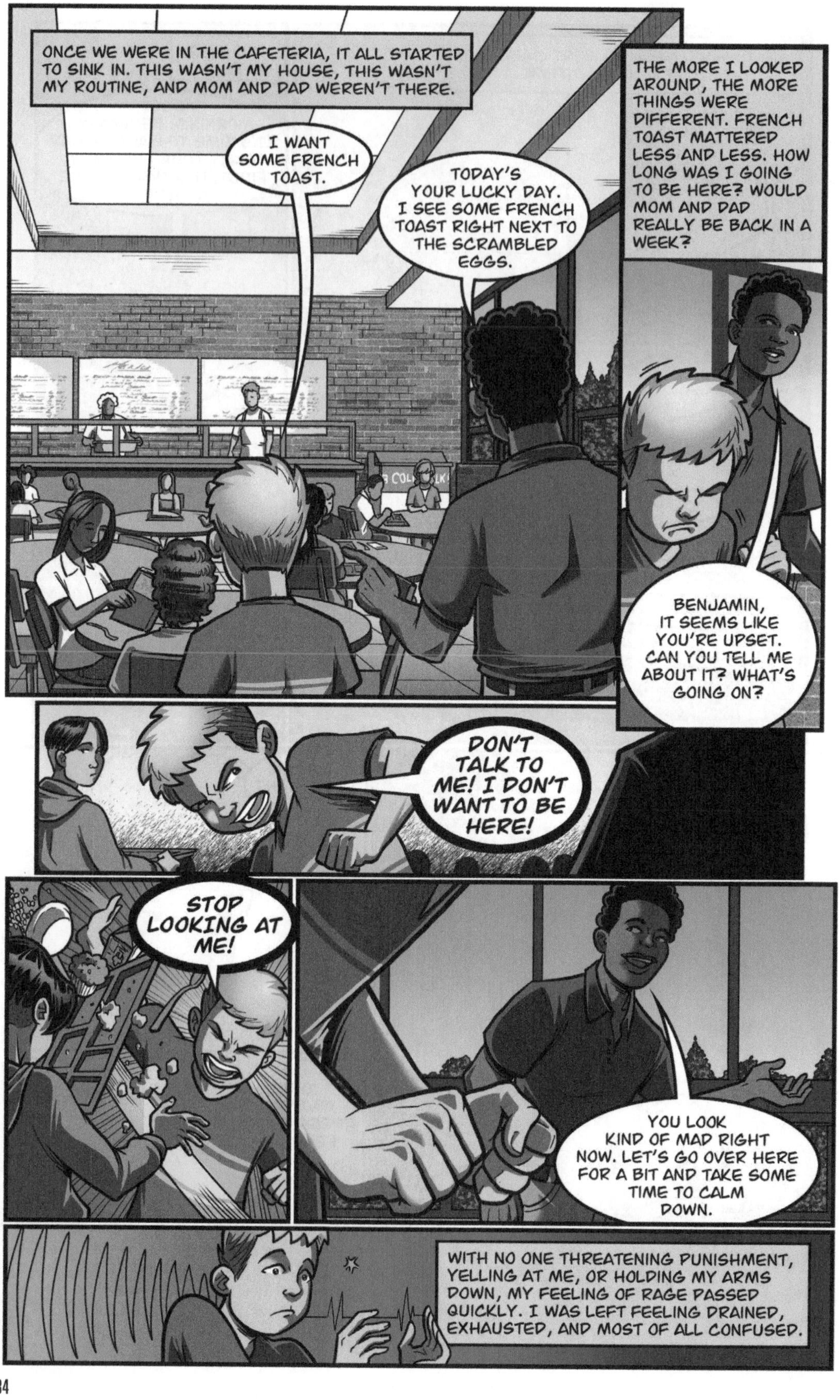
ONCE WE WERE IN THE CAFETERIA, IT ALL STARTED TO SINK IN. THIS WASN'T MY HOUSE, THIS WASN'T MY ROUTINE, AND MOM AND DAD WEREN'T THERE.
I WANT SOME FRENCH TOAST.
TODAY'S YOUR LUCKY DAY. I SEE SOME FRENCH TOAST RIGHT NEXT TO THE SCRAMBLED EGGS.
THE MORE I LOOKED AROUND, THE MORE THINGS WERE DIFFERENT. FRENCH TOAST MATTERED LESS AND LESS. HOW LONG WAS I GOING TO BE HERE? WOULD MOM AND DAD REALLY BE BACK IN A WEEK?
BENJAMIN, IT SEEMS LIKE YOU'RE UPSET. CAN YOU TELL ME ABOUT IT? WHAT'S GOING ON?
DON'T TALK TO ME! I DON'T WANT TO BE HERE!
STOP LOOKING AT ME!
YOU LOOK KIND OF MAD RIGHT NOW. LET'S GO OVER HERE FOR A BIT AND TAKE SOME TIME TO CALM DOWN.
WITH NO ONE THREATENING PUNISHMENT, YELLING AT ME, OR HOLDING MY ARMS DOWN, MY FEELING OF RAGE PASSED QUICKLY. I WAS LEFT FEELING DRAINED, EXHAUSTED, AND MOST OF ALL CONFUSED.

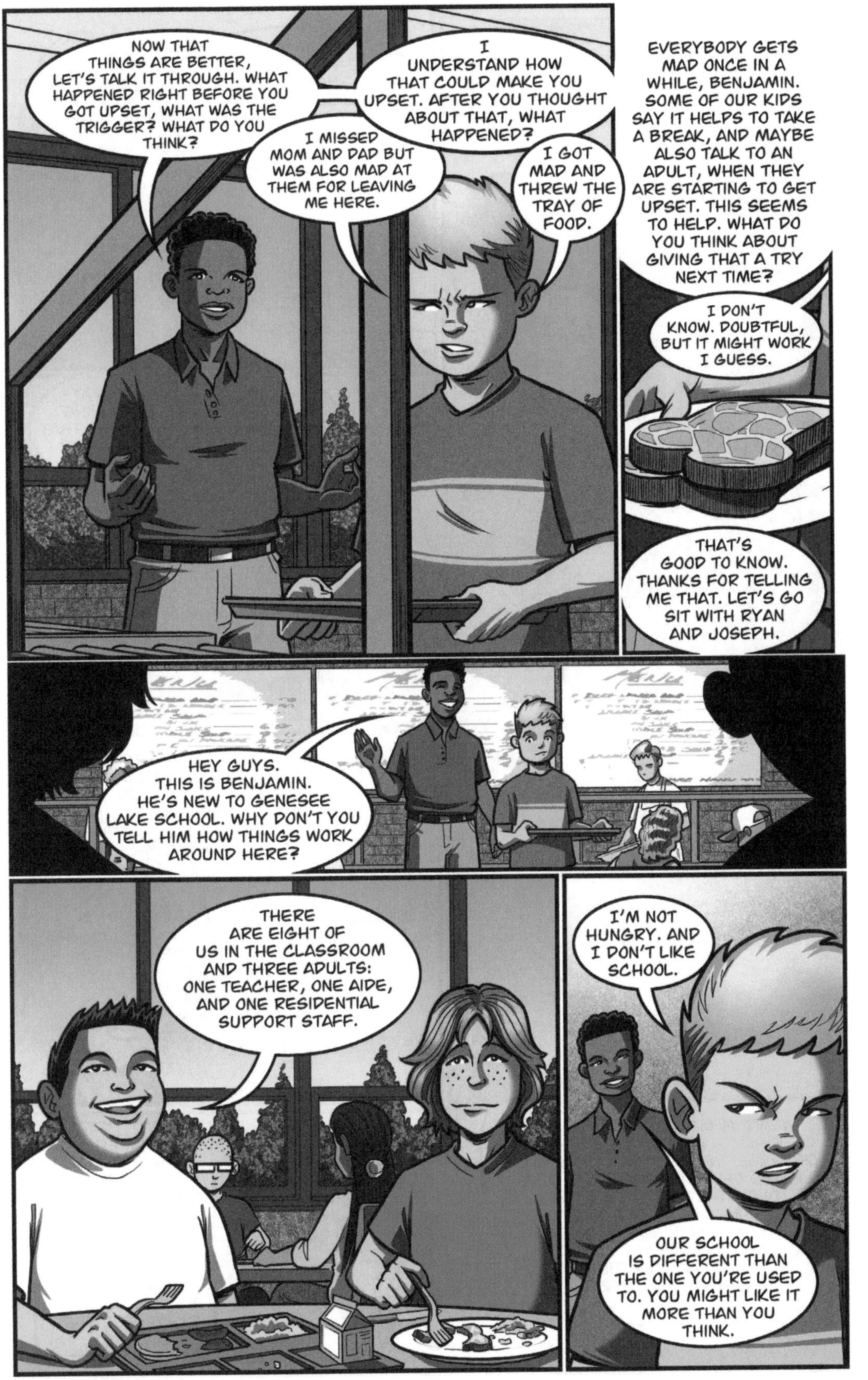
NOW THAT THINGS ARE BETTER, LET'S TALK IT THROUGH. WHAT HAPPENED RIGHT BEFORE YOU GOT UPSET, WHAT WAS THE TRIGGER? WHAT DO YOU THINK?
I MISSED MOM AND DAD BUT WAS ALSO MAD AT THEM FOR LEAVING ME HERE.
I UNDERSTAND HOW THAT COULD MAKE YOU UPSET. AFTER YOU THOUGHT ABOUT THAT, WHAT HAPPENED?
I GOT MAD AND THREW THE TRAY OF FOOD.
EVERYBODY GETS MAD ONCE IN A WHILE, BENJAMIN. SOME OF OUR KIDS SAY IT HELPS TO TAKE A BREAK, AND MAYBE ALSO TALK TO AN ADULT, WHEN THEY ARE STARTING TO GET UPSET. THIS SEEMS TO HELP. WHAT DO YOU THINK ABOUT GIVING THAT A TRY NEXT TIME?
I DON'T KNOW. DOUBTFUL, BUT IT MIGHT WORK I GUESS.
THAT'S GOOD TO KNOW. THANKS FOR TELLING ME THAT. LET'S GO SIT WITH RYAN AND JOSEPH.
HEY GUYS. THIS IS BENJAMIN. HE'S NEW TO GENESEE LAKE SCHOOL. WHY DON'T YOU TELL HIM HOW THINGS WORK AROUND HERE?
THERE ARE EIGHT OF US IN THE CLASSROOM AND THREE ADULTS: ONE TEACHER, ONE AIDE, AND ONE RESIDENTIAL SUPPORT STAFF.
I'M NOT HUNGRY. AND I DON'T LIKE SCHOOL.
OUR SCHOOL IS DIFFERENT THAN THE ONE YOU'RE USED TO. YOU MIGHT LIKE IT MORE THAN YOU THINK.

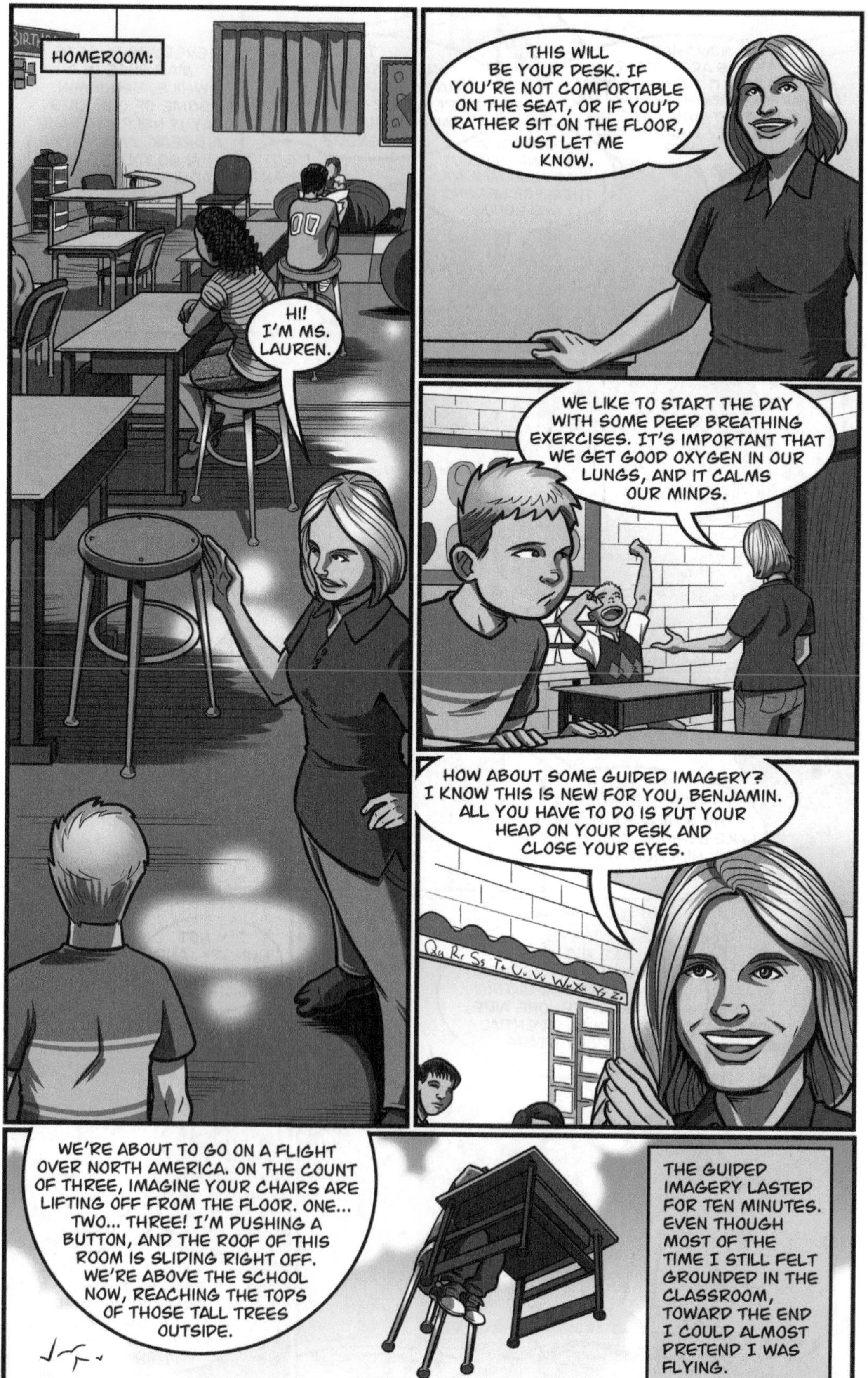
HOMEROOM:
HI! I'M MS. LAUREN.
THIS WILL BE YOUR DESK. IF YOU'RE NOT COMFORTABLE ON THE SEAT, OR IF YOU'D RATHER SIT ON THE FLOOR, JUST LET ME KNOW.
WE LIKE TO START THE DAY WITH SOME DEEP BREATHING EXERCISES. IT'S IMPORTANT THAT WE GET GOOD OXYGEN IN OUR LUNGS, AND IT CALMS OUR MINDS.
HOW ABOUT SOME GUIDED IMAGERY? I KNOW THIS IS NEW FOR YOU, BENJAMIN. ALL YOU HAVE TO DO IS PUT YOUR HEAD ON YOUR DESK AND CLOSE YOUR EYES.
WE'RE ABOUT TO GO ON A FLIGHT OVER NORTH AMERICA. ON THE COUNT OF THREE, IMAGINE YOUR CHAIRS ARE LIFTING OFF FROM THE FLOOR. ONE... TWO... THREE! I'M PUSHING A BUTTON, AND THE ROOF OF THIS ROOM IS SLIDING RIGHT OFF. WE'RE ABOVE THE SCHOOL NOW, REACHING THE TOPS OF THOSE TALL TREES OUTSIDE.
THE GUIDED IMAGERY LASTED FOR TEN MINUTES. EVEN THOUGH MOST OF THE TIME I STILL FELT GROUNDED IN THE CLASSROOM, TOWARD THE END I COULD ALMOST PRETEND I WAS FLYING.

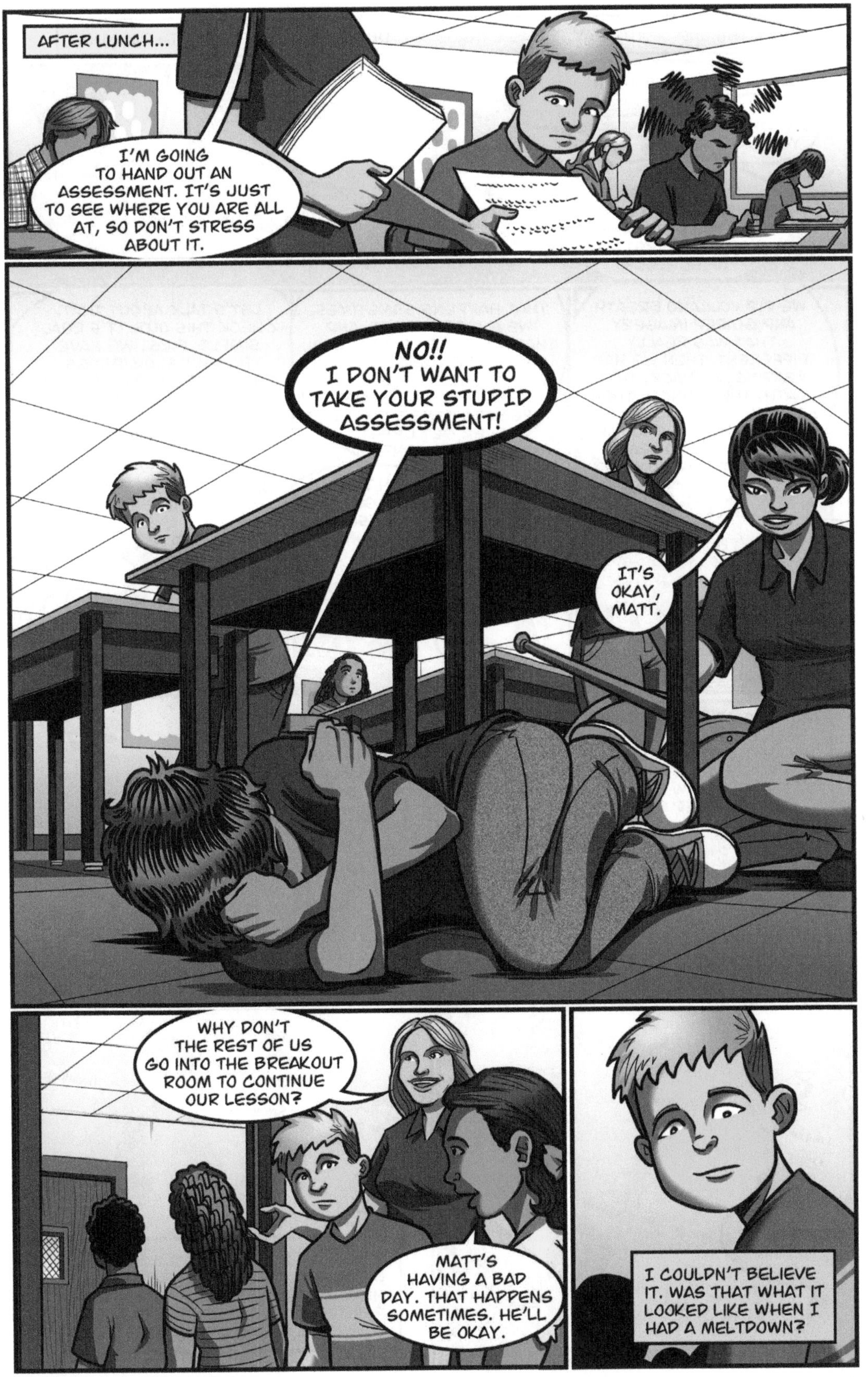
AFTER LUNCH...
I'M GOING TO HAND OUT AN ASSESSMENT. IT'S JUST TO SEE WHERE YOU ARE ALL AT, SO DON'T STRESS ABOUT IT.
NO!! I DON'T WANT TO TAKE YOUR STUPID ASSESSMENT!
IT'S OKAY, MATT.
WHY DON'T THE REST OF US GO INTO THE BREAKOUT ROOM TO CONTINUE OUR LESSON?
MATT'S HAVING A BAD DAY. THAT HAPPENS SOMETIMES. HE'LL BE OKAY.
I COULDN'T BELIEVE IT. WAS THAT WHAT IT LOOKED LIKE WHEN I HAD A MELTDOWN?

BY THE END OF THE DAY, I WAS EXHAUSTED, BUT I HAD A MEETING WITH DR. MIKE.

SIT ANYWHERE YOU LIKE.

I KNOW WE JUST MET, BUT I'D LIKE TO GET TO KNOW YOU BETTER. HOW WAS YOUR FIRST DAY OF SCHOOL?

WE DID VOLCANO BREATH AND GUIDED IMAGERY. THAT WAS REALLY DIFFERENT. THEN WE HAD READING, A SNACK, THEN MATH, THEN LUNCH, THEN SCIENCE. I LIKE SCIENCE. A BOY GOT ANGRY, THOUGH, AND WE HAD TO LEAVE THE CLASSROOM.

THAT HAPPENS SOMETIMES. WE ALL GET UPSET, AND THAT'S ALL RIGHT. YOU KNOW, THERE ARE THINGS WE CAN DO THAT HELP US WHEN WE GET UPSET OR START FEELING TENSE. DO YOU EVER GET UPSET, BENJAMIN?

OH YEAH. I CAN GET VERY UPSET.

LET'S TALK ABOUT THAT. CHECK THIS OUT. IT'S REAL SIMPLE. FIRST WE HAVE TRIGGERS, OR THINGS THAT HAPPEN TO MAKE YOU UPSET, THE SECOND PART HAS TO DO WITH HOW YOUR BODY FEELS AND REACTS, AND THE LAST PART IS ABOUT WHAT YOU AND WE CAN DO TO HELP YOU COPE AND FEEL BETTER.

DR. MIKE ASKED SOME QUESTIONS, AND WE FIGURED OUT THAT I GOT UPSET AT LOUD NOISES, SURPRISES, AND WHEN PEOPLE YELLED OR WERE MEAN. I HAD NEVER PAID ATTENTION TO WHAT UPSET ME BEFORE, BUT IT HELPED TO SEE THE PICTURES.

LOOK AT THE SECOND PART. CAN YOU TELL ME WHAT YOUR BODY FEELS LIKE WHEN YOU GET UPSET?

See

Too many people

Darkness

Someone being

touched

Yelling

Thunderstorms

Having a

Loud noises

Being surprised

Other

Being left alone

Not having visitors

Clench teeth

Loud voice

Red/hot face

Being mean or rude

Swearing

Racing heart

Breathing hard

I WOUND UP POINTING AT ALMOST ALL OF THE PICTURES—RED FACE, YELLING, HITTING, RUNNING AWAY. THE MORE I POINTED AT, THE WORSE I FELT. NO WONDER I WAS IN A SPECIAL SCHOOL.

IT SEEMS LIKE YOU MIGHT BE GETTING UPSET. IT'S ALL RIGHT. SOMETIMES IT'S TOUGH TO TALK ABOUT THESE THINGS, BUT IT IS IMPORTANT.

I DON'T WANT TO TALK TO YOU. I DON'T WANT TO TALK TO ANYONE.

Fidget tools

Games

Toys or Blocks

Stress ball or clay

Special blanket or cloth

Do Not Disturb

I KNOW IT'S HARD RIGHT NOW, BUT HOW ABOUT ONE LAST PAGE? THIS IS THE NEAT PART. THIS IS WHERE WE FIGURE OUT THE THINGS THAT MAKE YOU FEEL BETTER.

Watching TV

Looking at pictures

SQUEEZE BALLS, QUIET PLACES, AND TAKING WALKS SOMETIMES HELP.

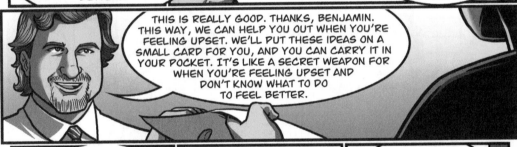

THIS IS REALLY GOOD. THANKS, BENJAMIN. THIS WAY, WE CAN HELP YOU OUT WHEN YOU'RE FEELING UPSET. WE'LL PUT THESE IDEAS ON A SMALL CARD FOR YOU, AND YOU CAN CARRY IT IN YOUR POCKET. IT'S LIKE A SECRET WEAPON FOR WHEN YOU'RE FEELING UPSET AND DON'T KNOW WHAT TO DO TO FEEL BETTER.

THERE ARE SOME KIDS YOUR AGE IN THE GYM. WE CAN CHECK THAT OUT BEFORE DINNER. I THINK YOU'D LIKE OUR SOCIAL PROBLEM-SOLVING GROUP.

I HATE GROUPS. I DID IT BEFORE, AND IT WAS AWFUL. THEY DIDN'T GIVE ME THE SAME STICKERS AS EVERYONE ELSE.

OUR GROUP IS DIFFERENT. IT'S IMPORTANT TO LEARN CERTAIN STEPS WHEN FIGURING OUT PROBLEMS AND HOW TO MAKE FRIENDS, BUT IT'S ALSO IMPORTANT TO HAVE FUN AND WORK ON TEAMWORK. WE LEARN TO THINK THINGS THROUGH BECAUSE IT MAKES IT EASIER FOR US TO SOLVE PROBLEMS. WE ALSO TALK ABOUT OUR COPING TOOLS AND COPING TOOLBOXES. LET'S GO MEET THE GUYS AND HANG OUT.

I DON'T WANT TO. I DON'T LIKE THESE KIDS. THEY'RE WEIRD, AND I DON'T LIKE BEING HERE. I WANT TO CALL MY MOM *NOW*.

ALL RIGHT, THEN. LET'S FIND MELANIE, AND WE'LL MAKE THAT CALL.

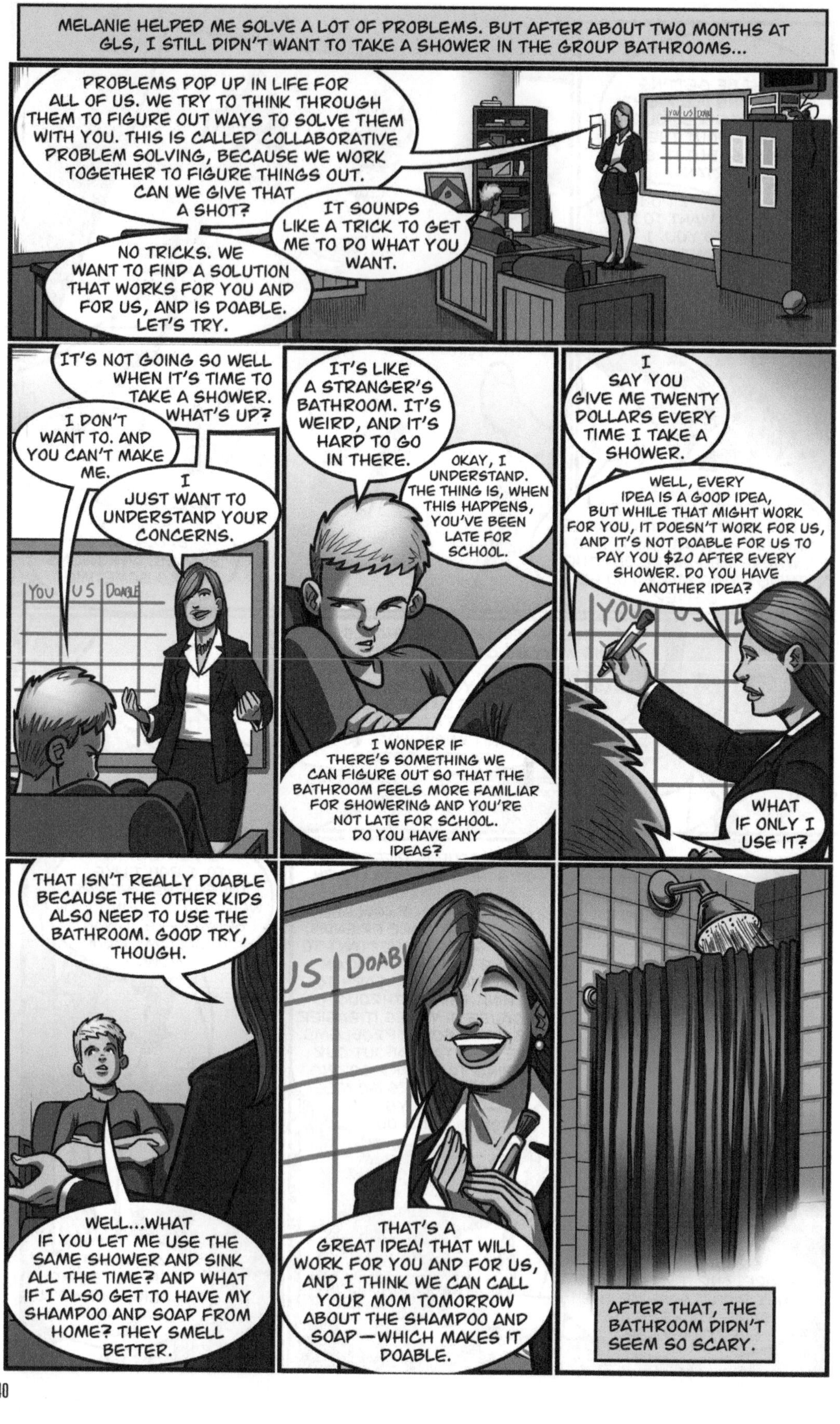
MELANIE HELPED ME SOLVE A LOT OF PROBLEMS. BUT AFTER ABOUT TWO MONTHS AT GLS, I STILL DIDN'T WANT TO TAKE A SHOWER IN THE GROUP BATHROOMS...
PROBLEMS POP UP IN LIFE FOR ALL OF US. WE TRY TO THINK THROUGH THEM TO FIGURE OUT WAYS TO SOLVE THEM WITH YOU. THIS IS CALLED COLLABORATIVE PROBLEM SOLVING, BECAUSE WE WORK TOGETHER TO FIGURE THINGS OUT. CAN WE GIVE THAT A SHOT?
IT SOUNDS LIKE A TRICK TO GET ME TO DO WHAT YOU WANT.
NO TRICKS. WE WANT TO FIND A SOLUTION THAT WORKS FOR YOU AND FOR US, AND IS DOABLE. LET'S TRY.
YOU US DOABLE
IT'S NOT GOING SO WELL WHEN IT'S TIME TO TAKE A SHOWER. WHAT'S UP?
I DON'T WANT TO. AND YOU CAN'T MAKE ME.
I JUST WANT TO UNDERSTAND YOUR CONCERNS.
YOU US DOABLE
IT'S LIKE A STRANGER'S BATHROOM. IT'S WEIRD, AND IT'S HARD TO GO IN THERE.
OKAY, I UNDERSTAND. THE THING IS, WHEN THIS HAPPENS, YOU'VE BEEN LATE FOR SCHOOL.
I WONDER IF THERE'S SOMETHING WE CAN FIGURE OUT SO THAT THE BATHROOM FEELS MORE FAMILIAR FOR SHOWERING AND YOU'RE NOT LATE FOR SCHOOL. DO YOU HAVE ANY IDEAS?
I SAY YOU GIVE ME TWENTY DOLLARS EVERY TIME I TAKE A SHOWER.
WELL, EVERY IDEA IS A GOOD IDEA, BUT WHILE THAT MIGHT WORK FOR YOU, IT DOESN'T WORK FOR US, AND IT'S NOT DOABLE FOR US TO PAY YOU $20 AFTER EVERY SHOWER. DO YOU HAVE ANOTHER IDEA?
WHAT IF ONLY I USE IT?
THAT ISN'T REALLY DOABLE BECAUSE THE OTHER KIDS ALSO NEED TO USE THE BATHROOM. GOOD TRY, THOUGH.
WELL...WHAT IF YOU LET ME USE THE SAME SHOWER AND SINK ALL THE TIME? AND WHAT IF I ALSO GET TO HAVE MY SHAMPOO AND SOAP FROM HOME? THEY SMELL BETTER.
US DOABL
THAT'S A GREAT IDEA! THAT WILL WORK FOR YOU AND FOR US, AND I THINK WE CAN CALL YOUR MOM TOMORROW ABOUT THE SHAMPOO AND SOAP—WHICH MAKES IT DOABLE.
AFTER THAT, THE BATHROOM DIDN'T SEEM SO SCARY.

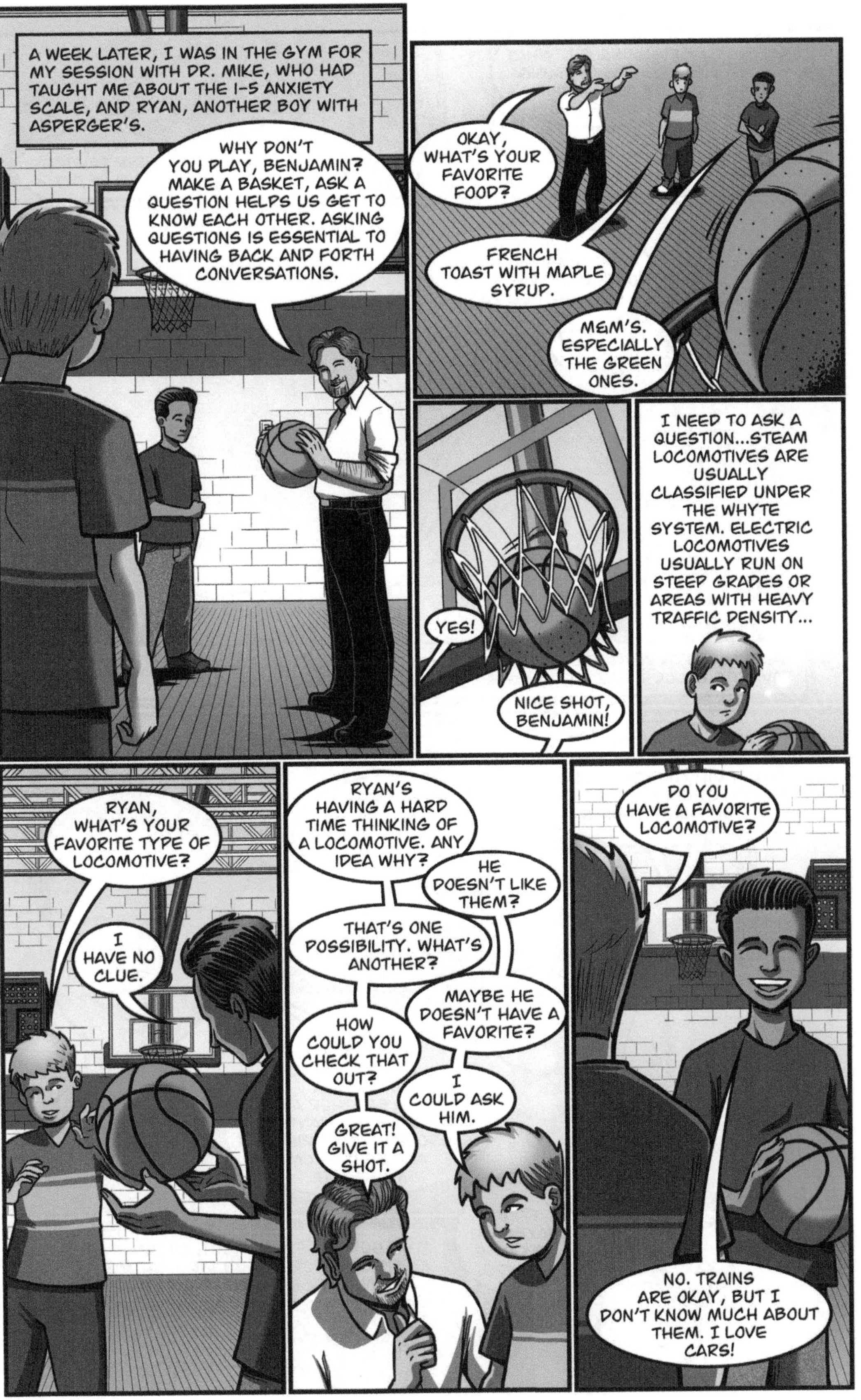
A WEEK LATER, I WAS IN THE GYM FOR MY SESSION WITH DR. MIKE, WHO HAD TAUGHT ME ABOUT THE 1-5 ANXIETY SCALE, AND RYAN, ANOTHER BOY WITH ASPERGER'S.
WHY DON'T YOU PLAY, BENJAMIN? MAKE A BASKET, ASK A QUESTION HELPS US GET TO KNOW EACH OTHER. ASKING QUESTIONS IS ESSENTIAL TO HAVING BACK AND FORTH CONVERSATIONS.
OKAY, WHAT'S YOUR FAVORITE FOOD?
FRENCH TOAST WITH MAPLE SYRUP.
M&M'S. ESPECIALLY THE GREEN ONES.
YES!
NICE SHOT, BENJAMIN!
I NEED TO ASK A QUESTION...STEAM LOCOMOTIVES ARE USUALLY CLASSIFIED UNDER THE WHYTE SYSTEM. ELECTRIC LOCOMOTIVES USUALLY RUN ON STEEP GRADES OR AREAS WITH HEAVY TRAFFIC DENSITY...
RYAN, WHAT'S YOUR FAVORITE TYPE OF LOCOMOTIVE?
I HAVE NO CLUE.
RYAN'S HAVING A HARD TIME THINKING OF A LOCOMOTIVE. ANY IDEA WHY?
HE DOESN'T LIKE THEM?
THAT'S ONE POSSIBILITY. WHAT'S ANOTHER?
MAYBE HE DOESN'T HAVE A FAVORITE?
HOW COULD YOU CHECK THAT OUT?
I COULD ASK HIM.
GREAT! GIVE IT A SHOT.
DO YOU HAVE A FAVORITE LOCOMOTIVE?
NO. TRAINS ARE OKAY, BUT I DON'T KNOW MUCH ABOUT THEM. I LOVE CARS!

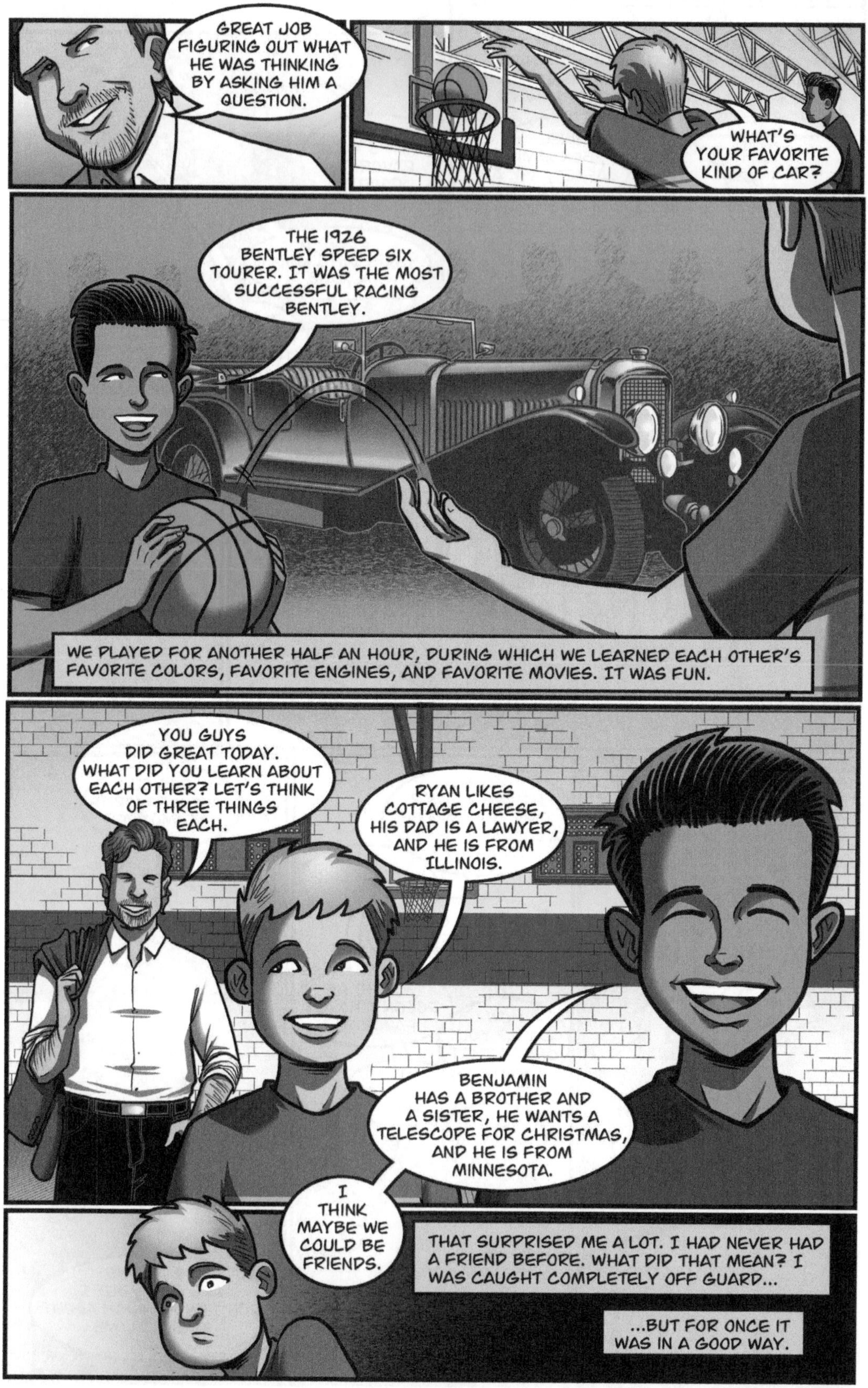
GREAT JOB FIGURING OUT WHAT HE WAS THINKING BY ASKING HIM A QUESTION.
WHAT'S YOUR FAVORITE KIND OF CAR?
THE 1926 BENTLEY SPEED SIX TOURER. IT WAS THE MOST SUCCESSFUL RACING BENTLEY.
WE PLAYED FOR ANOTHER HALF AN HOUR, DURING WHICH WE LEARNED EACH OTHER'S FAVORITE COLORS, FAVORITE ENGINES, AND FAVORITE MOVIES. IT WAS FUN.
YOU GUYS DID GREAT TODAY. WHAT DID YOU LEARN ABOUT EACH OTHER? LET'S THINK OF THREE THINGS EACH.
RYAN LIKES COTTAGE CHEESE, HIS DAD IS A LAWYER, AND HE IS FROM ILLINOIS.
BENJAMIN HAS A BROTHER AND A SISTER, HE WANTS A TELESCOPE FOR CHRISTMAS, AND HE IS FROM MINNESOTA.
I THINK MAYBE WE COULD BE FRIENDS.
THAT SURPRISED ME A LOT. I HAD NEVER HAD A FRIEND BEFORE. WHAT DID THAT MEAN? I WAS CAUGHT COMPLETELY OFF GUARD...
...BUT FOR ONCE IT WAS IN A GOOD WAY.

THE NEXT NIGHT, I WAS IN THE ACTIVITY ROOM. MELANIE TOLD ME THERE WAS A STEAM LOCOMOTIVE DOCUMENTARY ON TV, AND I HAD BEEN LOOKING FORWARD TO IT ALL DAY.
YOU'VE BEEN WATCHING YOUR TRAINS FOREVER. GIVE SOMEONE ELSE A TURN.
AUSTIN, THE SHOW IS OVER IN TEN MINUTES. YOU CAN WATCH WHAT YOU WANT AFTER.
IT'S MY TURN. BENJAMIN CAN GET OVER IT.
NO! IT'S FREE TIME! I GET TO SEE THE GOLDEN AGE OF STEAM!
CHANGE IT BACK! CHANGE IT BACK! CHANGE IT BACK!
WHAT'S GOING ON?
HE'S HOGGING THE TV, AND IT'S MY TURN!
DID YOU ASK IF HE WOULD SHARE?
NO.
BENJAMIN, YOU SEEM UPSET. REMEMBER THE COPING TOOLS WE TALKED ABOUT?
XIETY SC
5
Forget it. My self-contro is zero. I need help from someone.
4
It's pretty hard for me right now. My body feels wiry and tense, brain is getting fuzzy, and I need to take a break or take a walk with someone safe.
3
I'm okay. But I would li somebody nearby to support me.
2
I'm cool.
No problem. I'm in complete control.
GO FOR A WALK. I WANT TO GO FOR A WALK WITH YOU NOW.

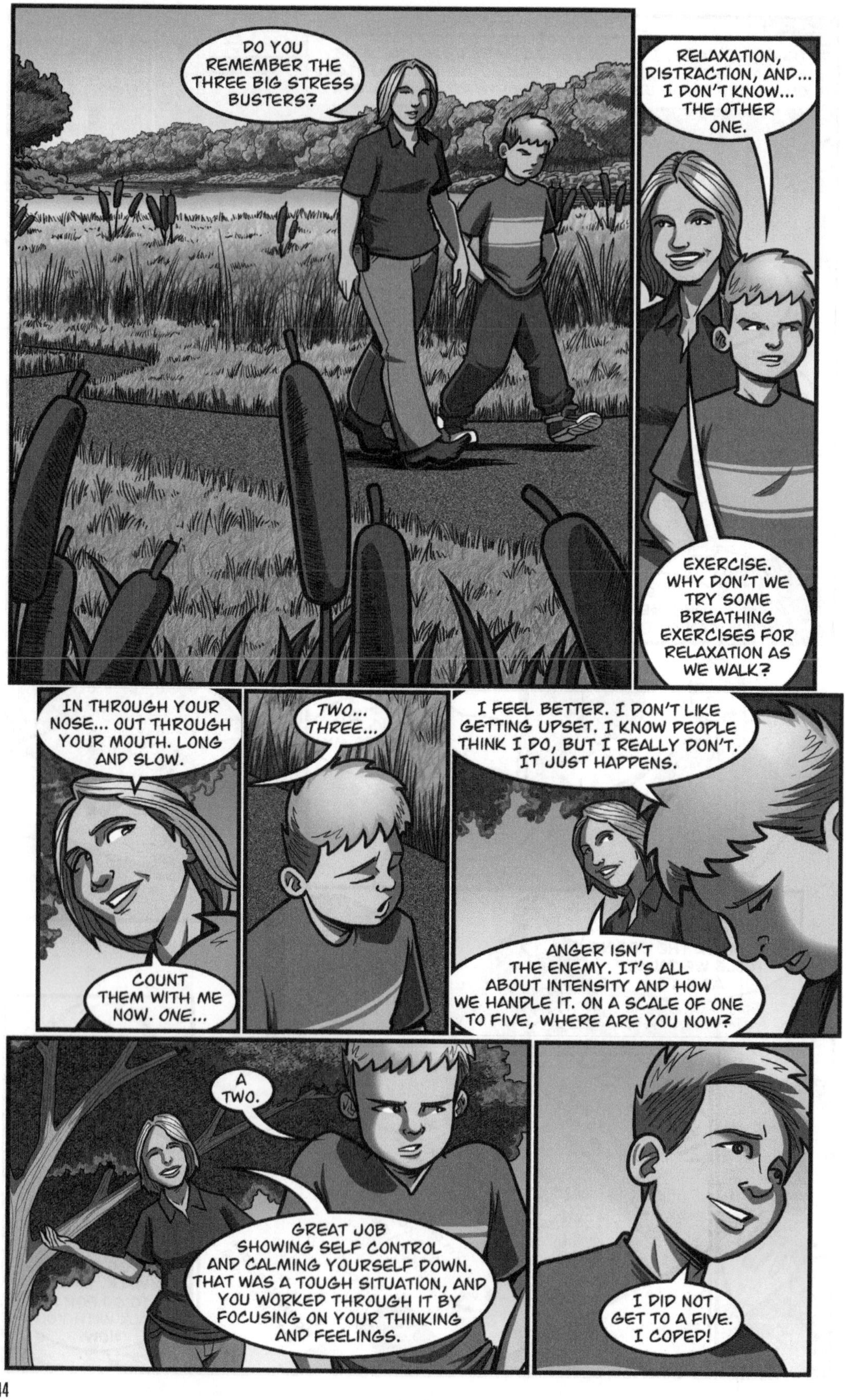
DO YOU REMEMBER THE THREE BIG STRESS BUSTERS?
RELAXATION, DISTRACTION, AND... I DON'T KNOW... THE OTHER ONE.
EXERCISE. WHY DON'T WE TRY SOME BREATHING EXERCISES FOR RELAXATION AS WE WALK?
IN THROUGH YOUR NOSE... OUT THROUGH YOUR MOUTH. LONG AND SLOW.
COUNT THEM WITH ME NOW. ONE...
TWO... THREE...
I FEEL BETTER. I DON'T LIKE GETTING UPSET. I KNOW PEOPLE THINK I DO, BUT I REALLY DON'T. IT JUST HAPPENS.
ANGER ISN'T THE ENEMY. IT'S ALL ABOUT INTENSITY AND HOW WE HANDLE IT. ON A SCALE OF ONE TO FIVE, WHERE ARE YOU NOW?
A TWO.
GREAT JOB SHOWING SELF CONTROL AND CALMING YOURSELF DOWN. THAT WAS A TOUGH SITUATION, AND YOU WORKED THROUGH IT BY FOCUSING ON YOUR THINKING AND FEELINGS.
I DID NOT GET TO A FIVE. I COPED!

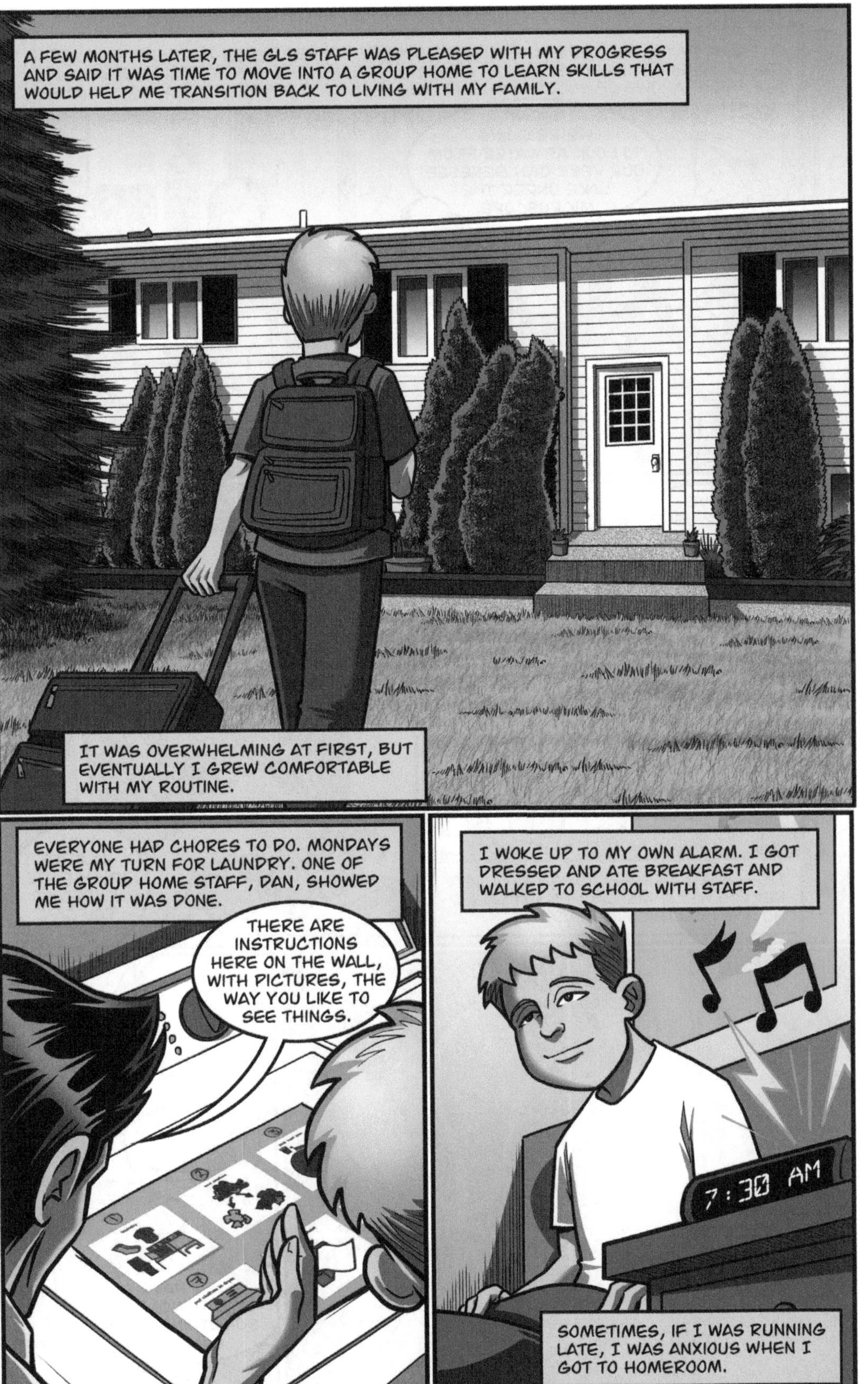
A FEW MONTHS LATER, THE GLS STAFF WAS PLEASED WITH MY PROGRESS AND SAID IT WAS TIME TO MOVE INTO A GROUP HOME TO LEARN SKILLS THAT WOULD HELP ME TRANSITION BACK TO LIVING WITH MY FAMILY.
IT WAS OVERWHELMING AT FIRST, BUT EVENTUALLY I GREW COMFORTABLE WITH MY ROUTINE.
EVERYONE HAD CHORES TO DO. MONDAYS WERE MY TURN FOR LAUNDRY. ONE OF THE GROUP HOME STAFF, DAN, SHOWED ME HOW IT WAS DONE.
THERE ARE INSTRUCTIONS HERE ON THE WALL, WITH PICTURES, THE WAY YOU LIKE TO SEE THINGS.
I WOKE UP TO MY OWN ALARM. I GOT DRESSED AND ATE BREAKFAST AND WALKED TO SCHOOL WITH STAFF.
7:30 AM
SOMETIMES, IF I WAS RUNNING LATE, I WAS ANXIOUS WHEN I GOT TO HOMEROOM.

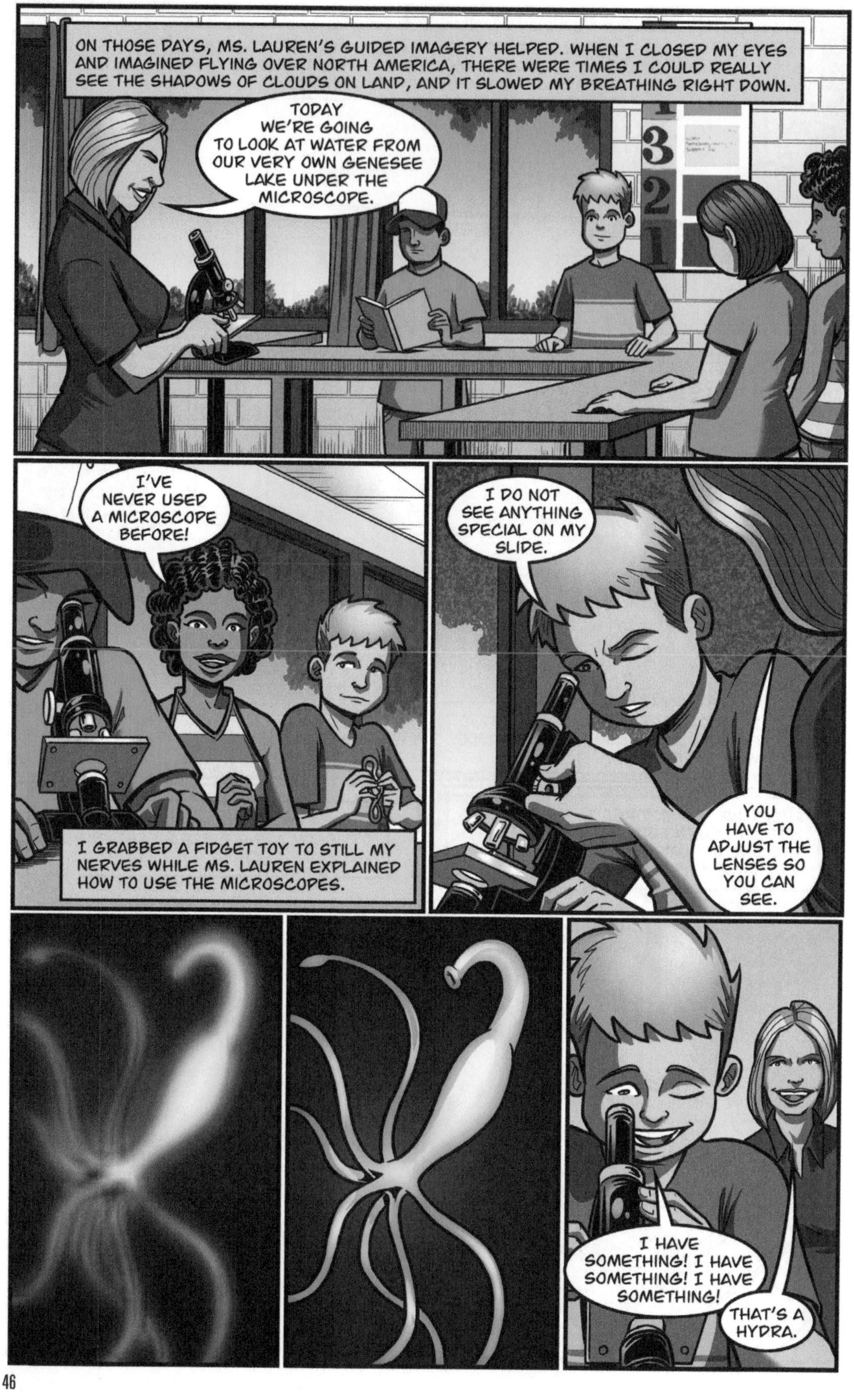
ON THOSE DAYS, MS. LAUREN'S GUIDED IMAGERY HELPED. WHEN I CLOSED MY EYES AND IMAGINED FLYING OVER NORTH AMERICA, THERE WERE TIMES I COULD REALLY SEE THE SHADOWS OF CLOUDS ON LAND, AND IT SLOWED MY BREATHING RIGHT DOWN.
TODAY WE'RE GOING TO LOOK AT WATER FROM OUR VERY OWN GENESEE LAKE UNDER THE MICROSCOPE.
I'VE NEVER USED A MICROSCOPE BEFORE!
I GRABBED A FIDGET TOY TO STILL MY NERVES WHILE MS. LAUREN EXPLAINED HOW TO USE THE MICROSCOPES.
I DO NOT SEE ANYTHING SPECIAL ON MY SLIDE.
YOU HAVE TO ADJUST THE LENSES SO YOU CAN SEE.
I HAVE SOMETHING! I HAVE SOMETHING! I HAVE SOMETHING!
THAT'S A HYDRA.

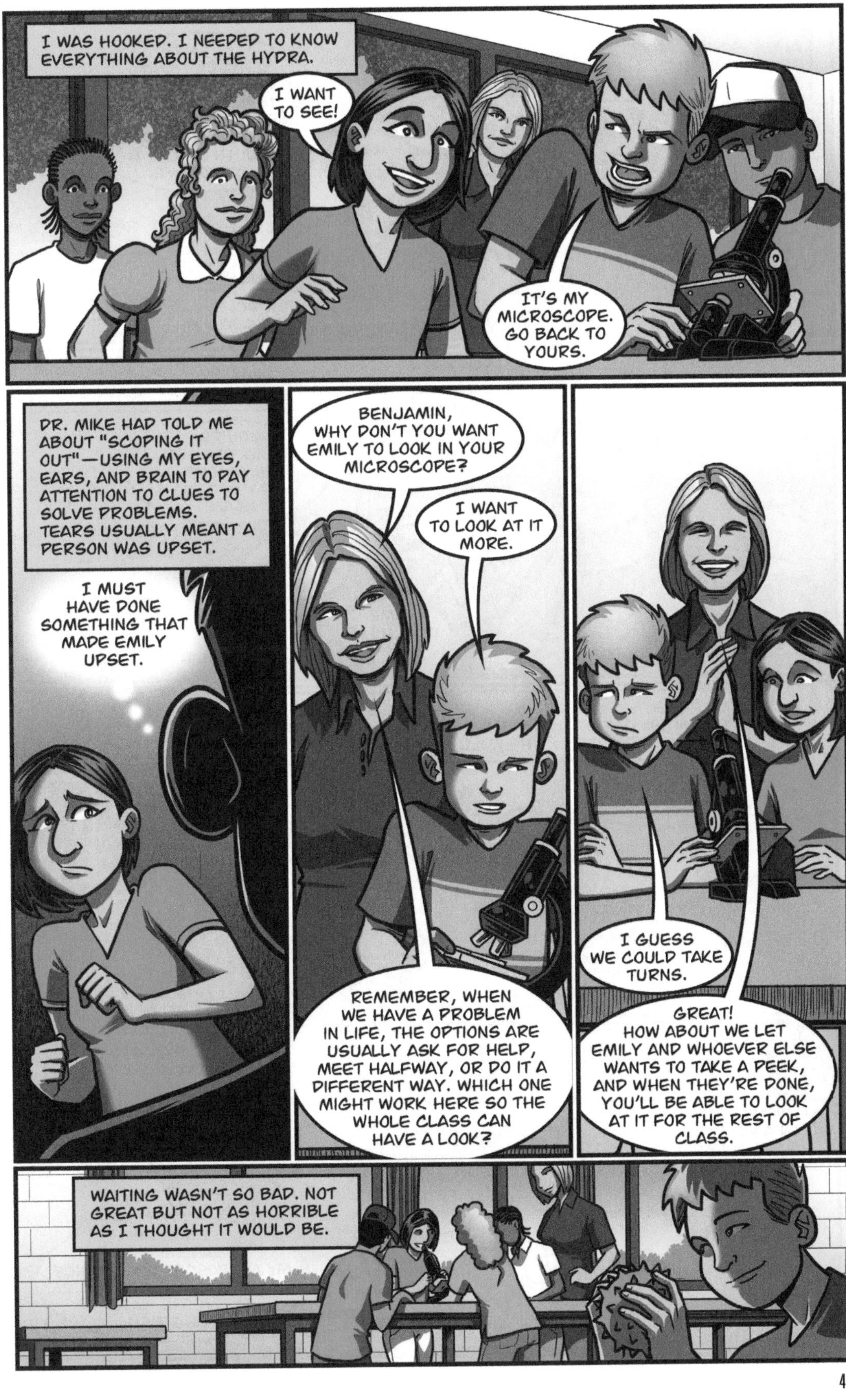

I WAS HOOKED. I NEEDED TO KNOW EVERYTHING ABOUT THE HYDRA.
I WANT TO SEE!
IT'S MY MICROSCOPE. GO BACK TO YOURS.
DR. MIKE HAD TOLD ME ABOUT "SCOPING IT OUT"—USING MY EYES, EARS, AND BRAIN TO PAY ATTENTION TO CLUES TO SOLVE PROBLEMS. TEARS USUALLY MEANT A PERSON WAS UPSET.
I MUST HAVE DONE SOMETHING THAT MADE EMILY UPSET.
BENJAMIN, WHY DON'T YOU WANT EMILY TO LOOK IN YOUR MICROSCOPE?
I WANT TO LOOK AT IT MORE.
REMEMBER, WHEN WE HAVE A PROBLEM IN LIFE, THE OPTIONS ARE USUALLY ASK FOR HELP, MEET HALFWAY, OR DO IT A DIFFERENT WAY. WHICH ONE MIGHT WORK HERE SO THE WHOLE CLASS CAN HAVE A LOOK?
I GUESS WE COULD TAKE TURNS.
GREAT! HOW ABOUT WE LET EMILY AND WHOEVER ELSE WANTS TO TAKE A PEEK, AND WHEN THEY'RE DONE, YOU'LL BE ABLE TO LOOK AT IT FOR THE REST OF CLASS.
WAITING WASN'T SO BAD. NOT GREAT BUT NOT AS HORRIBLE AS I THOUGHT IT WOULD BE.

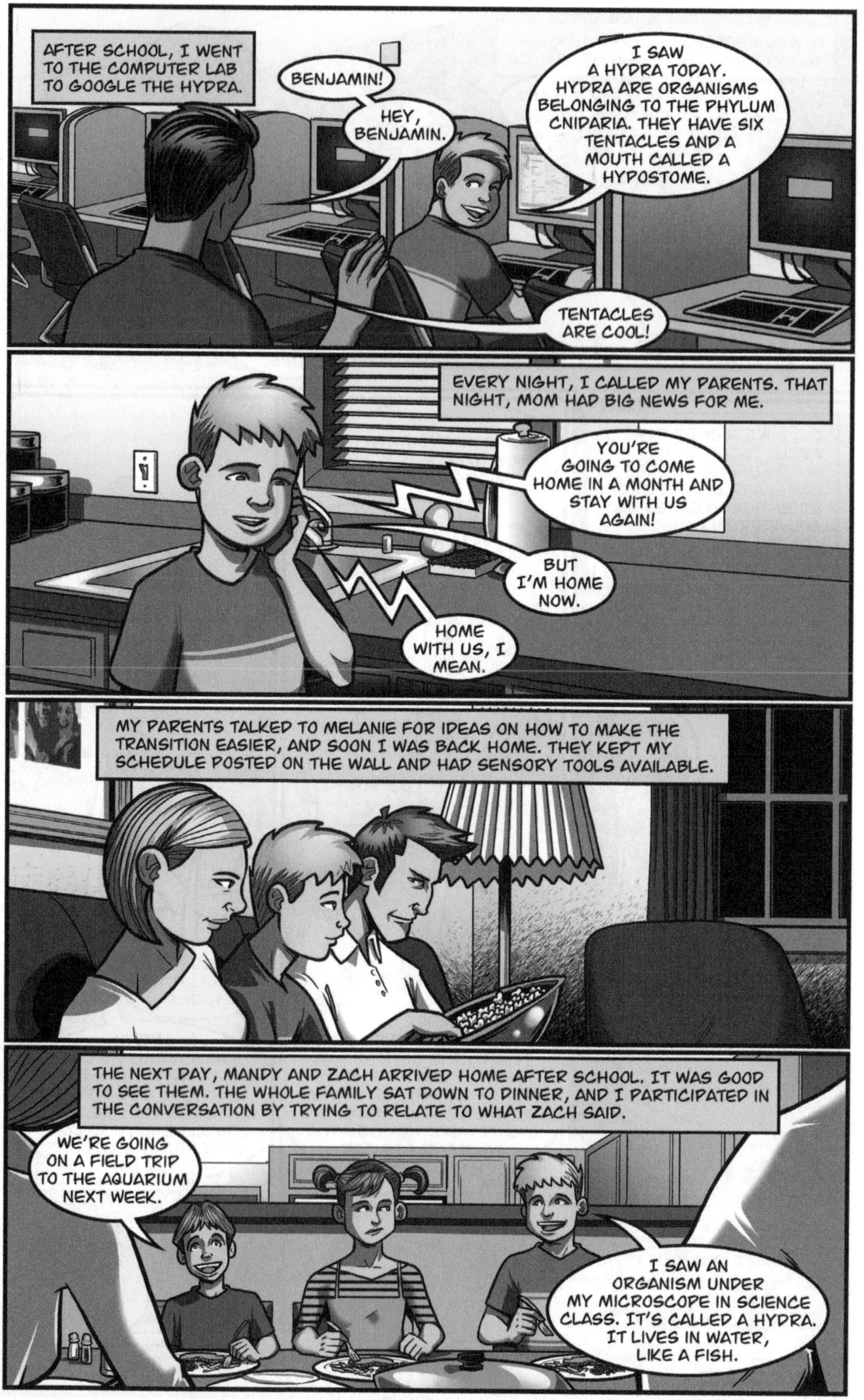
AFTER SCHOOL, I WENT TO THE COMPUTER LAB TO GOOGLE THE HYDRA.
BENJAMIN!
HEY, BENJAMIN.
I SAW A HYDRA TODAY. HYDRA ARE ORGANISMS BELONGING TO THE PHYLUM CNIDARIA. THEY HAVE SIX TENTACLES AND A MOUTH CALLED A HYPOSTOME.
TENTACLES ARE COOL!
EVERY NIGHT, I CALLED MY PARENTS. THAT NIGHT, MOM HAD BIG NEWS FOR ME.
YOU'RE GOING TO COME HOME IN A MONTH AND STAY WITH US AGAIN!
BUT I'M HOME NOW.
HOME WITH US, I MEAN.
MY PARENTS TALKED TO MELANIE FOR IDEAS ON HOW TO MAKE THE TRANSITION EASIER, AND SOON I WAS BACK HOME. THEY KEPT MY SCHEDULE POSTED ON THE WALL AND HAD SENSORY TOOLS AVAILABLE.
THE NEXT DAY, MANDY AND ZACH ARRIVED HOME AFTER SCHOOL. IT WAS GOOD TO SEE THEM. THE WHOLE FAMILY SAT DOWN TO DINNER, AND I PARTICIPATED IN THE CONVERSATION BY TRYING TO RELATE TO WHAT ZACH SAID.
WE'RE GOING ON A FIELD TRIP TO THE AQUARIUM NEXT WEEK.
I SAW AN ORGANISM UNDER MY MICROSCOPE IN SCIENCE CLASS. IT'S CALLED A HYDRA. IT LIVES IN WATER, LIKE A FISH.

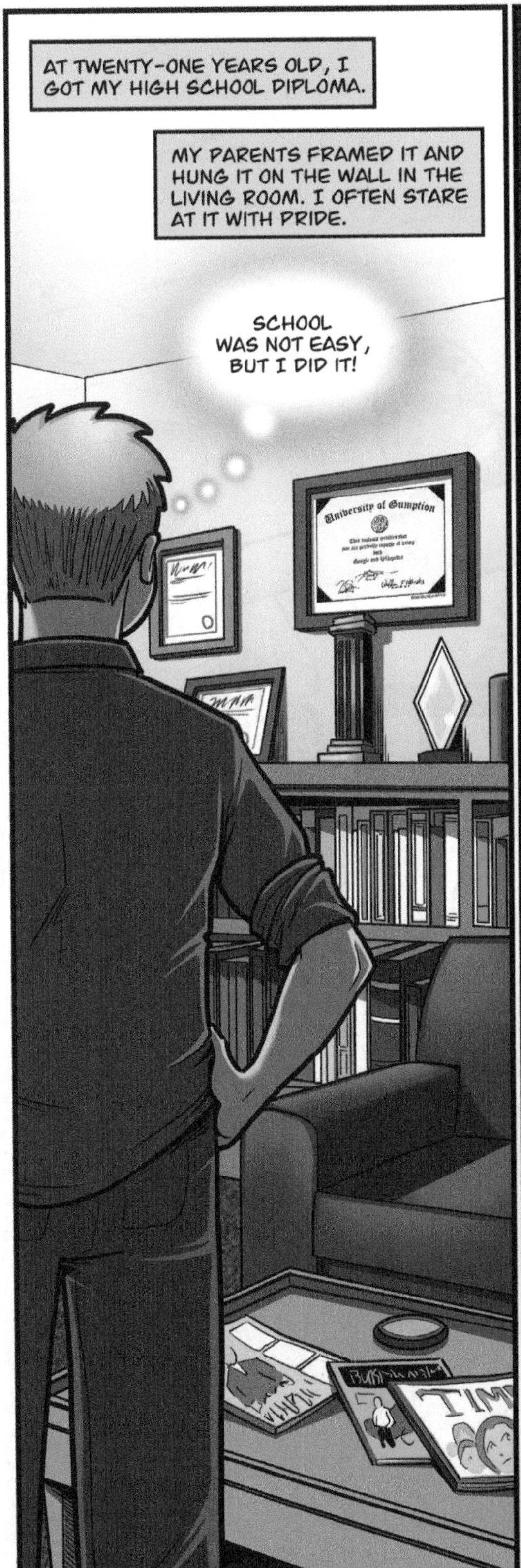

AT TWENTY-ONE YEARS OLD, I GOT MY HIGH SCHOOL DIPLOMA.
MY PARENTS FRAMED IT AND HUNG IT ON THE WALL IN THE LIVING ROOM. I OFTEN STARE AT IT WITH PRIDE.
SCHOOL WAS NOT EASY, BUT I DID IT!
University of Gumption
TIME

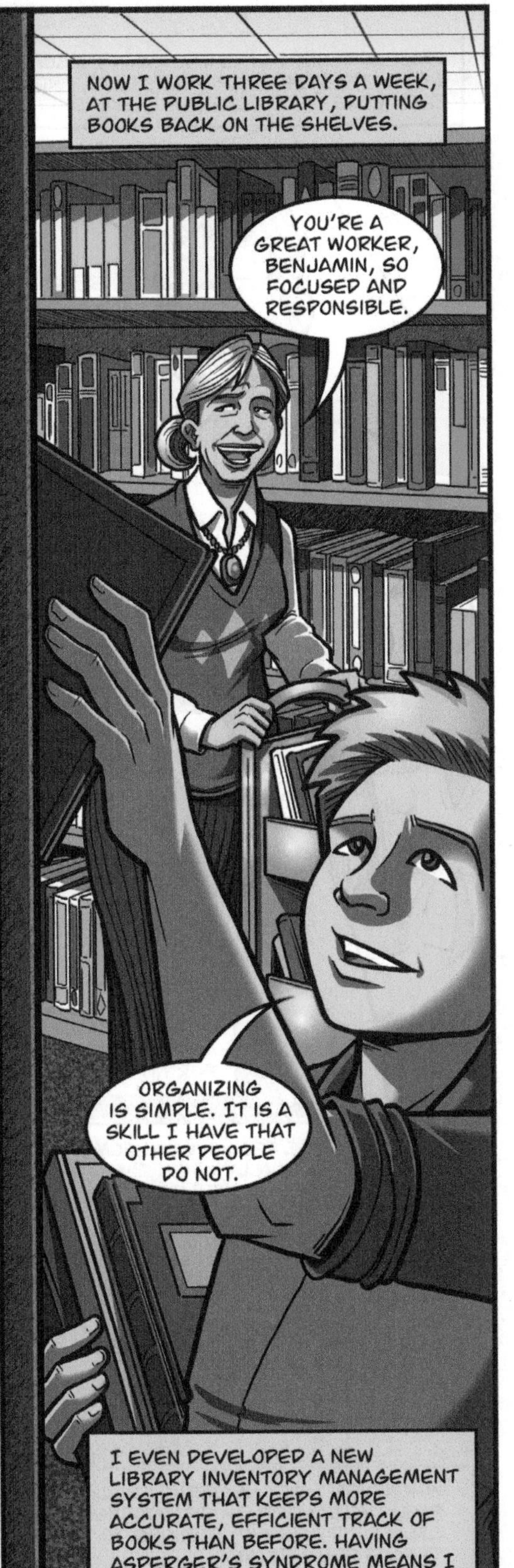

NOW I WORK THREE DAYS A WEEK, AT THE PUBLIC LIBRARY, PUTTING BOOKS BACK ON THE SHELVES.
YOU'RE A GREAT WORKER, BENJAMIN, SO FOCUSED AND RESPONSIBLE.
ORGANIZING IS SIMPLE. IT IS A SKILL I HAVE THAT OTHER PEOPLE DO NOT.
I EVEN DEVELOPED A NEW LIBRARY INVENTORY MANAGEMENT SYSTEM THAT KEEPS MORE ACCURATE, EFFICIENT TRACK OF BOOKS THAN BEFORE. HAVING ASPERGER'S SYNDROME MEANS I HAVE STRENGTHS, TOO, JUST LIKE EVERYONE ELSE.

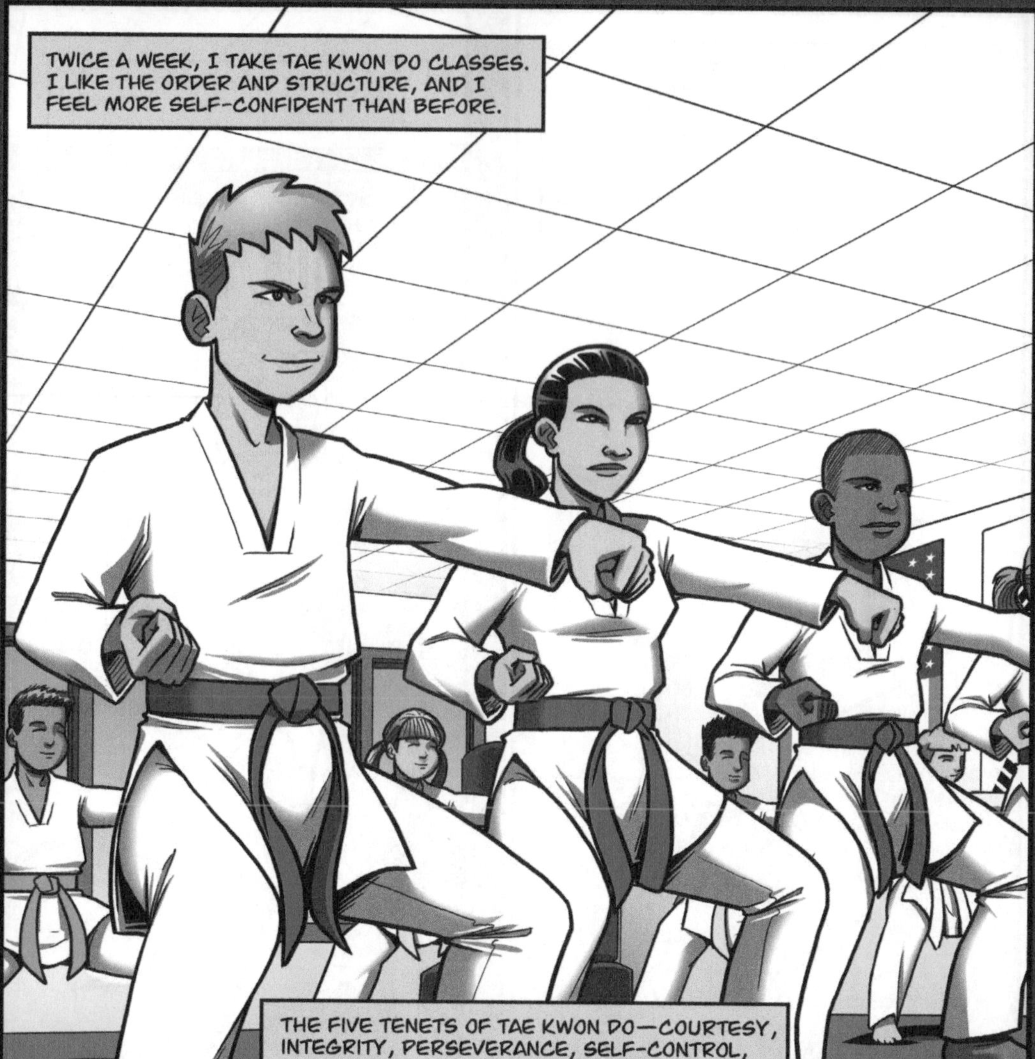
TWICE A WEEK, I TAKE TAE KWON DO CLASSES. I LIKE THE ORDER AND STRUCTURE, AND I FEEL MORE SELF-CONFIDENT THAN BEFORE.
THE FIVE TENETS OF TAE KWON DO—COURTESY, INTEGRITY, PERSEVERANCE, SELF-CONTROL, AND INDOMITABLE SPIRIT—ARE GOOD GUIDES FOR MY LIFE, ESPECIALLY SELF-CONTROL.

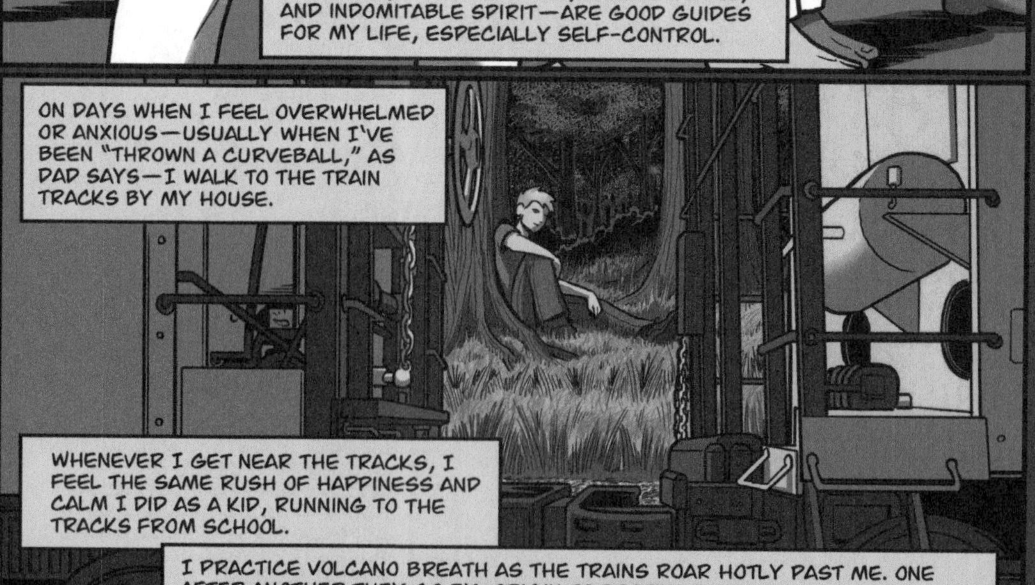
ON DAYS WHEN I FEEL OVERWHELMED OR ANXIOUS—USUALLY WHEN I'VE BEEN "THROWN A CURVEBALL," AS DAD SAYS—I WALK TO THE TRAIN TRACKS BY MY HOUSE.
WHENEVER I GET NEAR THE TRACKS, I FEEL THE SAME RUSH OF HAPPINESS AND CALM I DID AS A KID, RUNNING TO THE TRACKS FROM SCHOOL.
I PRACTICE VOLCANO BREATH AS THE TRAINS ROAR HOTLY PAST ME. ONE AFTER ANOTHER THEY GO BY, ORIGIN TO DESTINATION, ORIGIN TO DESTINATION.

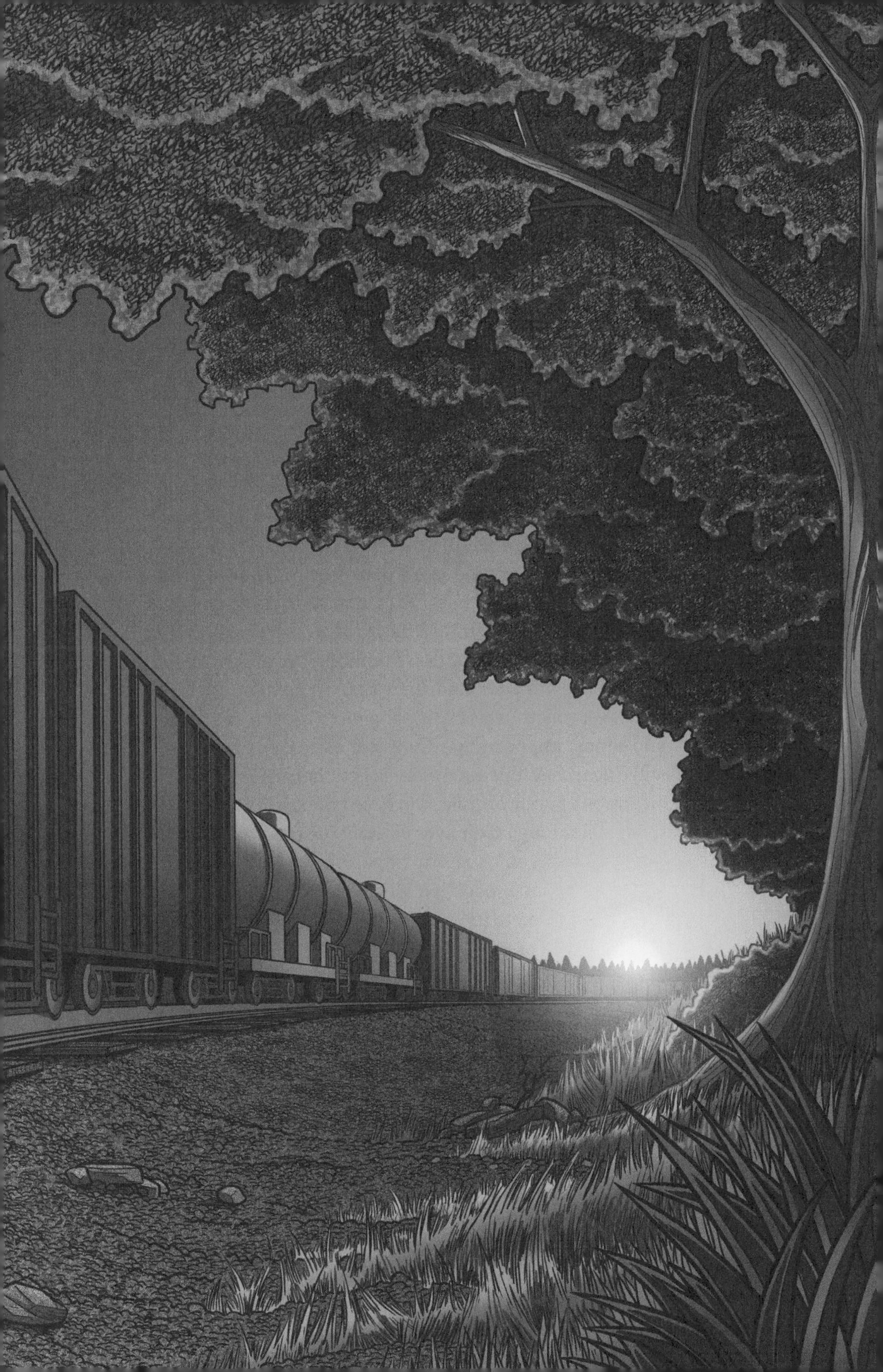

How These Books Were Created

The ORP Library of disabilities books is the result of heartfelt collaboration between numerous people: the staff of ORP, including the CEO, executive director, psychologists, clinical coordinators, teachers, and more; the families of children with disabilities served by ORP, including some of the children themselves; and the Round Table Companies (RTC) storytelling team. To create these books, RTC conducted dozens of intensive, intimate interviews over a period of months and performed independent research in order to truthfully and accurately depict the lives of these families. We are grateful to all those who donated their time in support of this message, generously sharing their experience, wisdom, and—most importantly—their stories so that the books will ring true. While each story is fictional and not based on any one family or child, we could not have envisioned the world through their eyes without the access we were so lovingly given. It is our hope that in reading this uniquely personal book, you felt the spirit of everyone who contributed to its creation.

Acknowledgments

The authors would like to thank the following team members at Genesee Lake School and ORP who generously lent their expertise to this book: science teacher Sheri Dunham, residential services director Sarah Goralski, admissions director Stephanie Koster-Peterson, and clinical coordinator supervisor Melissa Stoffel. Your time, perspective, passion, humor, and wisdom helped us bring this story to life—and help children like Benjamin every day.

We would also like to extend our heartfelt gratitude to the families who shared their journeys with us. The courage, ferocity, and love with which these parents shepherd their children through their lives is nothing short of heroic. Mark, Liz, Andy, and Kevin Blutstein; Susan Gallacci and Alex Spurgeon; Lois Menis, CJ Menis, and family; and the Taylors: Jeremy and Christian, and Hunter, Jacob, Jona, and Josh—thank you for inviting us into your stories. Your families are our inspiration.

And to readers of this book—the parents committed to helping their children, the educators who teach those children skills needed for independence, the therapists who shine a light on what can be a frighteningly mysterious road, and the schools and counties that make the difficult financial decisions that benefit these children—thank you. Your work is miraculous.

Resources

Attwood, Tony. *Asperger's Syndrome: A Guide for Parents and Professionals*. London, England: Jessica Kingsley Publishers, 1998.

Attwood, Tony. *The Complete Guide to Asperger's Syndrome*. London, England: Jessica Kingsley Publishers, 2007.

Buron, Kari D. & Curtis, Mitzi. *The Incredible 5-point Scale: Assisting Students with Autism Spectrum Disorders in Understanding Social interactions and Controlling Their Emotional Responses*. Shawnee Mission, KS: Autism Asperger Publishing Co., 2003.

Clark, Rick. "Cognitive Experiential Group Therapy" (Workshop presented at ODTC, Oconomowoc, Wisconsin, December 19, 2011).

Gray, Carol. *Comic Strip Conversations*. Arlington, TX: Future Horizons, 1994.

Greene, Ross W. *The Explosive Child*. New York: Harper Collins Publishers, 2005.

Greene, Ross W., and Ablon, J. Stuart. *Treating Explosive Kids: The Collaborative Problem-Solving Approach*. New York: The Guilford Press, 2006.

Greenspan, Stanley, and Wieder, Serena. *Engaging Autism: Using the Floortime Approach to Help Children Relate, Communicate, and Think*. Cambridge, MA.: Da Capo Press, 2006.

Smith Myles, Brenda, and Southwick, Jack. *Asperger Syndrome and Difficult Moments: Practical Solutions for Tantrums, Rage, and Meltdowns*. Shawnee Mission, KS: AAPC, 2005.

"Autism Internet Modules," *http://www.autisminternetmodules.org.*

"Interdisciplinary Council on Developmental and Learning Disorders," *http://www.icdl.com.*

"IDEA – Building the Legacy: IDEA 2004," *http://idea.ed.gov.*

"Massachusetts Department of Mental Health-Restraint/Seclusion Reduction Initiative: Safety Tool," *http://www.mass.gov/dmh/rsri.*

"Think:Kids, Rethinking Challenging Kids," *http://www.thinkkids.org.*

Nadja Baer

BIOGRAPHY

Nadja has been a words-nerd all her life. She speaks English, German, Italian, and Spanish (with varying degrees of fluency), can teach Tae Kwon Do classes in Korean, and is currently working on expanding her French vocabulary. Since receiving a Bachelor's degree in Creative Writing at the University of Minnesota, she has served as the office thesaurus, dictionary, translator, and spell-checker in every one of her day jobs. She wrote her first terrible novella at the age of eight, and is now focused on writing comics and novels for young adults. Her work can be seen for free in the online graphic novel, *Impure Blood* (*www.impurebloodwebcomic.com*), which is drawn by her husband. Other projects she has scripted for Round Table include *Everything's Okay* (Sept 2011) and *Delivering Happiness* (March 2012). Aside from a love of a good story with pretty pictures, they share a house, a cat, a turtle, and a belief that more people should embrace their inner nerd.

Nathan Lueth

BIOGRAPHY

Nathan came into existence with a pencil in his hand, a feat that continues to confound obstetricians to this day. No one knows for sure when he started drawing or where his love of comics came from, but most experts agree that his professional career began after graduating from the Minneapolis College of Art and Design, as a caricaturist in the Mall of America. Soon he was freelance illustrating for the likes of Target, General Mills, and Stone Arch Books.

When not drawing comics for other people, Nathan draws his own super awesome fantasy webcomic, *Impure Blood*. He is proud to be a part of Round Table Companies, as he believes that comics should be for everyone, not just nerds (it should be noted that he may be trying to turn the general population into nerds). He currently resides in St. Paul, Minnesota, with two cats, a turtle, and his wife, Nadja, upon whom he performs his nerd conversion experiments.

Jeffrey D. Krukar, Ph.D.

BIOGRAPHY

Jeffrey D. Krukar, Ph.D. is a licensed psychologist and certified school psychologist with more than 20 years of experience working with children and families in a variety of settings, including community based group homes, vocational rehabilitation services, residential treatment, juvenile corrections, public schools, and private practice. He earned his Ph.D. in educational psychology, with a school psychology specialization and psychology minor, from the University of Wisconsin-Milwaukee. Dr. Krukar is a registrant of the National Register of Health Service Providers in Psychology, and is also a member of the American Psychological Association.

As the psychologist at Genesee Lake School in Oconomowoc, WI, Dr. Krukar believes it truly takes a village to raise a child—to strengthen developmental foundations in relating, communicating, and thinking—so they can successfully return to their families and communities. Dr. Krukar hopes the ORP Library of disabilities books will bring to light the stories of children and families to a world that is generally not aware of their challenges and successes, as well as offer a sense of hope to those currently on this journey. His deepest hope is that some of the concepts in these books resonate with parents and professionals working with kids with disabilities, and offer possibilities that will help kids achieve their maximum potential and life enjoyment.

Katie Gutierrez

BIOGRAPHY

Katie Gutierrez believes that a well-told story can transcend what a reader "knows" to be real about the world—and thus change the world for that reader. In every form, story is transformative, and Katie is proud to spend her days immersed in it as executive editor for Round Table Companies, Inc.

Since 2007, Katie has edited approximately 50 books and co-written six—including *Meltdown*, one of the ORP Library of disabilities books. She has been humbled by the stories she has heard and hopes these books will help guide families on their often-lonely journeys, connecting them with resources and support. She also hopes they will give the general population a glimpse into the Herculean jobs taken on so fiercely by parents, doctors, therapists, educators, and others who live with, work with, and love children such as Benjamin.

Katie holds a BA in English and philosophy from Southwestern University and an MFA in fiction from Texas State University. She has contributed to or been profiled in publications including *Forbes*, *Entrepreneur* magazine, *People* magazine, *Hispanic Executive Quarterly*, and *Narrative* magazine. She can't believe she's lucky enough to do what she loves every day.

James G. Balestrieri

BIOGRAPHY

James G. Balestrieri is currently the CEO of Oconomowoc Residential Programs, Inc. (ORP). He has worked in the human services field for 40 years, holding positions that run the gamut to include assistant maintenance, assistant cook, direct care worker, teacher's aide, summer camp counselor, bookkeeper, business administrator, marketing director, CFO, and CEO. Jim graduated from Marquette University with a B.S. in Business Administration (1977) and a Master's in Business Administration with an emphasis in Marketing (1988). He is also a Certified Public Accountant (Wisconsin—1982). Jim has a passion for creatively addressing the needs of those with impairments by managing the inherent stress among funding, programming, and profitability. He believes that those with a disability enjoy rights and protections that were created by the hard-fought efforts of those who came before them; that the Civil Rights movement is not just for minority groups; and that people with disabilities have a right to find their place in the world and to achieve their maximum potential as individuals. For more information, see *www.orp.com*.

About ORP

Oconomowoc Residential Programs, Inc. is an employee-owned family of companies whose mission is to make a difference in the lives of people with disabilities. Our dedicated staff of 2,000 employee owners provides quality services and professional care to more than 1,700 children, adolescents, and adults with special needs. ORP provides a continuum of care, including residential therapeutic education, community-based residential services, support services, respite care, treatment programs, and day services. The individuals in our care include people with developmental disabilities, physical disabilities, and intellectual disabilities. **Our guiding principle is passion:** a passion for the people we serve and for the work we do. For a comprehensive look at our programs and people, please visit *www.orp.com*.

ORP offers two residential therapeutic education programs and one alternative day school among its array of services. These programs offer developmentally appropriate education and treatment for children, adolescents, and young adults in settings specially attuned to their needs. We provide special programs for students with specific academic and social issues relative to a wide range of disabilities, including autistic disorder, Asperger's disorder, mental retardation, anxiety disorders, depression, bipolar disorder, reactive attachment disorder, attention deficit disorder, Prader-Willi Syndrome, and other disabilities.

Genesee Lake School is a nationally recognized provider of comprehensive residential treatment, educational, and vocational services for children, adolescents, and young adults with emotional, mental health, neurological, or developmental disabilities. GLS has specific expertise in Autism Spectrum Disorders, anxiety and mood disorders, and behavioral disorders. We provide an individualized, person-centered, integrated team approach, which emphasizes positive behavioral support, therapeutic relationships, and developmentally appropriate practices. Our goal is to assist each individual to acquire skills to live, learn, and succeed in a community-based, less restrictive environment. GLS is particularly known for its high quality educational services for residential and day school students.

Genesee Lake School / Admissions Director
36100 Genesee Lake Road
Oconomowoc, WI 53066
262-569-5510
http://www.geneseelakeschool.com

T.C. Harris School is located in an attractive setting in Lafayette, Indiana. T.C. Harris teaches skills to last a lifetime, through a full therapeutic program as well as day school and other services.

T.C. Harris School / Admissions Director
3700 Rome Drive
Lafayette, IN 47905
765-448-4220
http://tcharrisschool.com

The Richardson School is a day school in West Allis, Wisconsin that provides an effective, positive alternative education environment serving children from Milwaukee and the surrounding communities.

The Richardson School / Director
6753 West Roger Street
West Allis, WI 53219
414-540-8500
http://www.richardsonschool.com

REACTIVE ATTACHMENT DISORDER

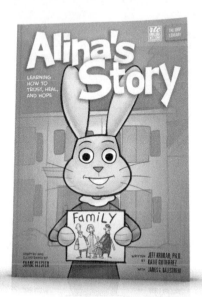

AN UNLIKELY TRUST

Alina's Story
LEARNING HOW TO TRUST, HEAL, AND HOPE
FamiLY

AN UNLIKELY TRUST

ALINA'S STORY OF ADOPTION, COMPLEX TRAUMA, HEALING, AND HOPE

ALINA'S STORY

LEARNING HOW TO TRUST, HEAL, AND HOPE

An Unlikely Trust: Alina's Story of Adoption, Complex Trauma, Healing, and Hope, and its companion children's book, *Alina's Story*, share the journey of Alina, a young girl adopted from Russia. After living in an orphanage during her early life, Alina is unequipped to cope with the complexities of the outside world. She has a deep mistrust of others and finds it difficult to talk about her feelings. When she is frightened, overwhelmed, or confused, she lashes out in rages that scare her family. Alina's parents know she needs help and work endlessly to find it for her, eventually discovering a special school that will teach Alina new skills. Slowly, Alina gets better at expressing her feelings and solving problems. For the first time in her life, she realizes she is truly safe and loved . . . and capable of loving in return.

ASPERGER'S DISORDER

THE ORP LIBRARY
MELTDOWN
ASPERGER'S DISORDER, CHALLENGING BEHAVIOR, AND A FAMILY'S JOURNEY TOWARD HOPE
Written by
JEFF KRUKAR, PH.D.
KATIE GUTIERREZ
with
JAMES G. BALESTRIERI

THE ORP LIBRARY
Melting Down
JEFF KRUKAR, PH.D.
KATIE GUTIERREZ
JAMES G. BALESTRIERI
NADJA BAER
NATHAN LUETH

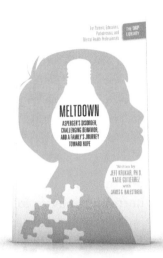

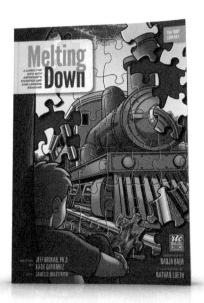

MELTDOWN

ASPERGER'S DISORDER, CHALLENGING BEHAVIOR, AND A FAMILY'S JOURNEY TOWARD HOPE

MELTING DOWN

A COMIC FOR KIDS WITH ASPERGER'S DISORDER AND CHALLENGING BEHAVIOR

Meltdown and its companion comic book, *Melting Down*, are both based on the fictional story of Benjamin, a boy diagnosed with Asperger's disorder and additional challenging behavior. From the time Benjamin is a toddler, he and his parents know he is different: he doesn't play with his sister, refuses to make eye contact, and doesn't communicate well with others. And his tantrums are not like normal tantrums; they're meltdowns that will eventually make regular schooling—and day-to-day life—impossible. Both the prose book, intended for parents, educators, and mental health professionals, and the comic for the kids themselves demonstrate that the journey toward hope isn't simple . . . but with the right tools and teammates, it's possible.

AUTISM SPECTRUM DISORDER

Mr. Incredible shares the fictional story of Adam, a boy diagnosed with autistic disorder. On Adam's first birthday, his mother recognizes that something is different about him: he recoils from the touch of his family, preferring to accept physical contact only in the cool water of the family's pool. As Adam grows older, he avoids eye contact, is largely nonverbal, and has very specific ways of getting through the day; when those habits are disrupted, intense meltdowns and self-harmful behavior follow. From seeking a diagnosis to advocating for special education services, from keeping Adam safe to discovering his strengths, his family becomes his biggest champion. The journey to realizing Adam's potential isn't easy, but with hope, love, and the right tools and teammates, they find that Adam truly is *Mr. Incredible.* The companion comic in this series, inspired by social stories, offers an innovative, dynamic way to guide children— and parents, educators, and caregivers—through some of the daily struggles experienced by those with autism.

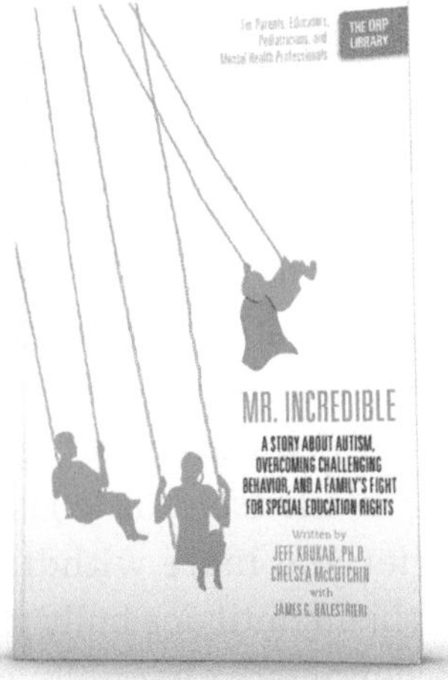
THE ORP LIBRARY
MR. INCREDIBLE
A STORY ABOUT AUTISM, OVERCOMING CHALLENGING BEHAVIOR, AND A FAMILY'S FIGHT FOR SPECIAL EDUCATION RIGHTS
Written by
JEFF KRUKAR, PH.D.
CHELSEA McCUTCHIN
with
JAMES G. BALESTRIERI

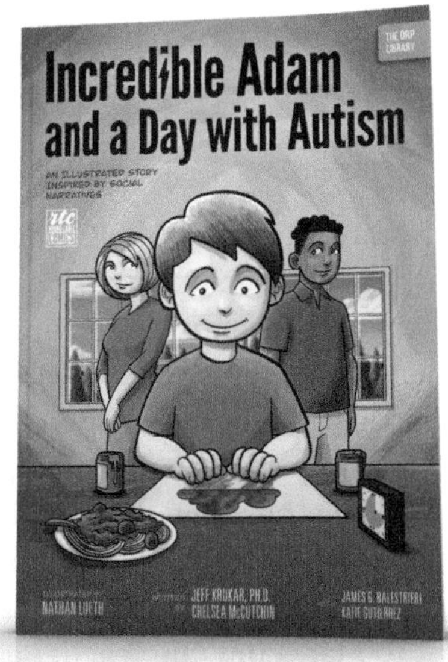
THE ORP LIBRARY
Incredible Adam and a Day with Autism
AN ILLUSTRATED STORY INSPIRED BY SOCIAL NARRATIVES
NATHAN LUETH
JEFF KRUKAR, PH.D.
CHELSEA McCUTCHIN
JAMES G. BALESTRIERI
KATIE GUTIERREZ

MR. INCREDIBLE

A STORY ABOUT AUTISM, OVERCOMING CHALLENGING BEHAVIOR, AND A FAMILY'S FIGHT FOR SPECIAL EDUCATION RIGHTS

INCREDIBLE ADAM AND A DAY WITH AUTISM

AN ILLUSTRATED STORY INSPIRED BY SOCIAL NARRATIVES

BULLYING

Nearly one third of all school children face physical, verbal, cyber, and social bullying on a regular basis. For years, educators and parents have searched for ways to end bullying, but as that behavior becomes more sophisticated, it's harder to recognize and to stop. In *Classroom Heroes* and its companion comic book, Jason is a quiet, socially awkward seventh grade boy who has long suffered bullying in silence. While Jason's parents notice him becoming angrier and more withdrawn, they don't realize the scope of the problem until one bully takes it too far—and one teacher acts on her determination to stop it. Both *Classroom Heroes* and its companion comic recognize that in order to stop bullying, we must change our mindset. We must enlist not only parents and educators but the children themselves to create a community that simply does not tolerate bullying. Jason's story demonstrates both the heartbreaking effects of bullying and the simple yet profound strategies to end it, one student at a time.

THE ORP LIBRARY
CLASSROOM HEROES
ONE CHILD'S STRUGGLE WITH BULLYING AND A TEACHER'S MISSION TO CHANGE SCHOOL CULTURE
Written by
JEFF KRUKAR, PH.D.
PAMELA DeLOATCH
with

CLASSROOM HEROES

ONE CHILD'S STRUGGLE
WITH BULLYING AND
A TEACHER'S MISSION TO
CHANGE SCHOOL CULTURE

Coming Soon

CLASSROOM HEROES

COMPANION CHILDREN'S BOOK

FAMILY SUPPORT

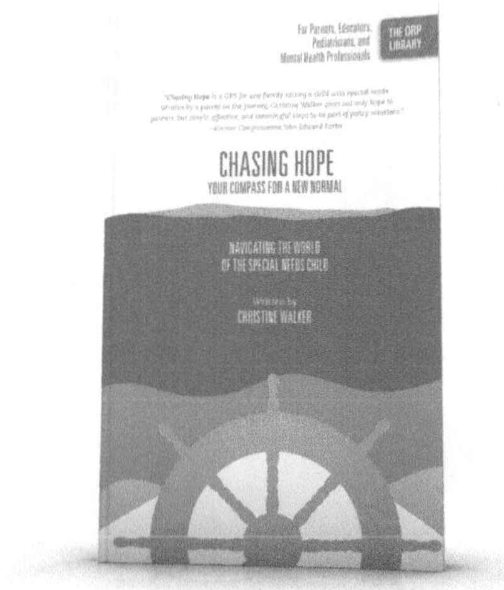
THE ORP
LIBRARY
CHASING HOPE
YOUR COMPASS FOR A NEW NORMAL
NAVIGATING THE WORLD
OF THE SPECIAL NEEDS CHILD
CHRISTINE WALKER

CHASING HOPE
YOUR COMPASS FOR A NEW NORMAL
NAVIGATING THE WORLD OF THE SPECIAL NEEDS CHILD

Schuyler Walker was just four years old when he was diagnosed with autism, bipolar disorder, and ADHD. In 2004, childhood mental illness was rarely talked about or understood. With knowledge and resources scarce, Schuyler's mom, Christine, navigated a lonely maze to determine what treatments, medications, and therapies could benefit her son. In the ten years since his diagnosis, Christine has often wished she had a "how to" guide that would provide the real mom-to-mom information she needed to survive the day and, in the end, help her family navigate the maze with knowledge, humor, grace, and love. Christine may not have had a manual at the beginning of her journey, but she hopes this book will serve as yours.

Also look for books on Prader-Willi Syndrome and children and psychotropic medications coming soon!

CPSIA information can be obtained at www.ICGtesting.com
Printed in the USA
BVOW11s1614010414

349302BV00002B/2/P